SIGNS OF THE JUDGEMENT, ONOMASTICA SACRA AND THE GENERATIONS FROM ADAM

University of Pennsylvania
Armenian Texts and Studies

Supported by the Sarkes Tarzian Fund

Editor
Michael E. Stone

Number 3

SIGNS OF THE JUDGEMENT,
ONOMASTICA SACRA AND
THE GENERATIONS FROM ADAM

SIGNS OF THE JUDGEMENT, ONOMASTICA SACRA AND THE GENERATIONS FROM ADAM

by
Michael E. Stone

SCHOLARS PRESS

Distributed by
Scholars Press
PO Box 2268
101 Salem St.
Chico, CA. 95927

236.9
Si26

82040122

SIGNS OF THE JUDGEMENT, ONOMASTICA SACRA AND THE GENERATIONS FROM ADAM

by

Michael E. Stone

Library of Congress Cataloging in Publication Data
Main entry under title:

Signs of the judgement, Onomastica sacra, and The
generations from Adam.

(University of Pennsylvania Armenian texts and
studies ; no. 3)
Latin, Armenian, and Hebrew texts, with
accompanying English translation for the latter two.
Includes bibliographical references and indexes.
1. Judgement Day. 2. Bible—Names. 3.
Bible—Chronology. 4. Bible—Genealogy. I. Stone, Michael
E., 1938- . II. Series: Pennsylvania. University.
University of Pennsylvania Armenian texts and studies ;
no. 3.
BT880.S56   236'.9   80-28371

ISBN 0-89130-460-6
ISBN 0-89130-461-4 (pbk.)

Printed in the United States of America

1   2   3   4   5

Edwards Brothers, Inc.
Ann Arbor, Michigan 48104

Dedicated to

GERSHOM G. SCHOLEM

whose learning and understanding have
guided and inspired me.

TABLE OF CONTENTS

The four writings published in this volume share two traits. The first is the diversity of their character. In the course of arranging the texts planned for inclusion in other volumes of Armenian pseudepigraphical texts, it became apparent that certain documents fitted naturally into none of them. Yet they were of inherent interest and it was therefore decided to gather them in a volume of their own, a volume to be typified by the variety of the documents which comprise it.

The second trait, perhaps a correlative of the first, is that not all of these texts are of the exact types usually included in collections of "Apocrypha and Pseudepigrapha". Indeed, in recent years it has come to be recognized that the body of so-called pseudepigrapha is not a fixed canon. To the contrary, it has become broadened and extended to comprehend a wide range of earlier and later crystallizations of traditions concerning biblical texts, personalities, and events. [1] Moreover, the study of the Armenian pseudepigrapha must properly include texts which are important for the understanding of the development of these biblical traditions among the Armenians.

These observations are particularly relevant to two of the documents published here, Onomastica Sacra Armeniaca and The Generations of Adam. They clearly apper-

---

1. On terminology see: A.-M Denis, Introduction aux Pseudepigraphes grecs de l'A.T. (Studia in Veteris Testamenti Pseudepigrapha, I), Leiden 1970, p. xi. A clear example of this extended use of the term is evident in the range of works included in the Pseudepigrapha Series of Texts and Translations. See most recently J. H. Charlesworth, The Pseudepigrapha and Modern Research (SCS 7;Missoula, S.P. 1976) 17,28.

tain to the development of biblical traditions, but are
not formally of the type usually included under the ru-
bric "Apocrypha and Pseudepigrapha". Their position in
the present volume, nonetheless, flows clearly from the
considerations set forth above.

The other two works, The Signs of the Judgement and
The Peoples of the Sons of Noah are of more familiar
types and their affiliation of the Apocrypha and Pseudepigrapha is immediately evident.

The four documents are of varying degrees of interest, and their chief characteristics are set forth in
the "Introductory Remarks". In the case of one, The
Signs of Judgement, its existence in various European
tongues and the discovery of a previously unrecognized
Hebrew translation, as well as its great intrinsic interest, required a particularly extensive discussion.
Another, Onomastica Sacra Armeniaca, is extant in so
many manuscripts and types that it was feasible to publish only part of them in full.

The various texts from Armenian manuscripts in the
Library of the Armenian Patriarchate in Jerusalem, the
Library of the Mechitarist Fathers in Venice, the Bibliothèque Nationale in Paris and the Matenadaran in Erevan
are published by permission of the Librarians of those
centers of learning. The Hebrew text from Bodl. MS.Heb.
d 11 (fol. 257r and v) is published by permission of
the Keeper of Oriental Books,the Bodleian Library.

The author is particularly indebted to the judic-
ious and learned counsel and unfailing encouragement of
Archbishop Norayr Bogharian, Librarian of Manuscripts of
the Armenian Patriarchate in Jerusalem.

The Israel Academy of Science and Humanities, the
Research Funds of the Hebrew University of Jerusalem and
the Tarzian Chair of Armenian History and Culture of the
University of Pennsylvania have all proffered material
support in the preparation of this book.

Michael E. Stone   Jerusalem, 1980

MANUSCRIPTS PUBLISHED HERE FOR THE FIRST TIME

ARMENIAN

Erevan

No. 533,   p. 234   Sons of Noah   1660

No. 2261, fols. 300v ff.   Onomastica   XVII century

No. 8076, fols. 221r-222r   Generations of   XVII century
                              Adam

Jerusalem

No. 657,   fols. 285r ff.   Onomastica   no date

No. 857,   fols. 101r ff.   Onomastica   no date

No. 1008, fols. 1 r ff.   Onomastica   no date

No. 1173, fols. 3r ff.   Onomastica   XVII century

No. 1352, pp. 297 ff.   Onomastica   1688

No. 1372, pp. 29 ff.   Onomastica   no date

No. 1422, fols. 325r ff.   Onomastica   XVII century

No. 1448, fols. 263r ff.   Onomastica   1583

No. 1666, fols. 97r ff.   Onomastica   1642

No. 1672, fols. 5 ff.   Onomastica   XVII century

No. 1682, fols. 185 ff.   Onomastica   1359

No. 1699, pp. 10 ff.   Onomastica   XVII century

No. 1912, pp. 7 ff.   Onomastica   no date

No. 2481, pp. 123 ff.   Onomastica   XIII century

Paris, Bibliothèque Nationale

Cod, Arm. 140 fols. 239v ff. Onomastica   no date

Venice, Mechitarist Fathers

No. 39,   pp. 120 ff.   Onomastica   no date

No. 544,   pp. 1 ff.   Onomastica   XVI-XVII centuries

No. 1409, pp. 1 ff.   Onomastica   no date

HEBREW

Oxford, Bodleian Library

Cod. Heb d 11   fols. 257r-257v The Signs   XIV century

TRANSCRIPTION OF THE ARMENIAN ALPHABET

Ա ա	Բ բ	Գ գ	Դ դ	Ե ե	Զ զ	Է է	Ը ը	Թ թ	Ժ ժ	Ի ի
A	B	G	D	E	Z	Ē	Ĕ	T'	Ž	I
Լ լ	Խ խ	Ծ ծ	Կ կ	Հ հ	Ձ ձ	Ղ ղ	Ճ ճ	Մ մ	Յ յ	Ն ն
L	X	C	K	H	J	Ł	Č	M	Y	N
Շ շ	Ո ո	Չ չ	Պ պ	Ջ ջ	Ռ ռ	Ս ս	Վ վ	Տ տ	Ր ր	Ց ց
Š	O	Č'	P	J̌	Ṙ	S	V	T	R	C'
Ւ ւ	Փ փ	Ք ք	Օ օ	Ֆ ֆ						
W	P'	K'	Ō	F						

BIBLIOGRAPHICAL ABBREVIATIONS

Aleppo Catalogue

A. Surmēyan, Catalogue des manuscrits armeniens se trouvant a Alep a l'Eglise des Quarante Martyrs, Jerusalem: St. James Press, 1935(Armenian)

Amalyan   H.M. Amalyan, Mediaeval Armenian Glossaries (5th-15th centuries), Erevan: Academy of Sciences, 1966 (Armenian).

Ap. Elijah

J.M. Rosenstiehl, L'Apocalypse d'Elie (Textes et Etudes pour ... judaisme intertestamentaire, 1), Paris: Geuthner, 1972.

Apocalypse of Thomas

M.R. James, The Apocryphal New Testament, Oxford: 1955, pp. 555-562.

Arm. 4 Ezra

M.E. Stone, The Armenian Version of 4 Ezra (Pennsylvania Armenian Texts and Studies, 1) Missoula: Scholars Press, 1978.

Berlin Catalogue

N. Karamianz, Verzeichniss der armenischen Handschriften der koeniglichen Bibliothek zu Berlin, Berlin: Asher, 1888.

Bodleian Catalogue

S. Baronian & F.C. Conybeare, Catalogue of the Armenian Manuscripts in the Bodleian Library, Oxford: 1918.

Book of John the Evangelist

M.R. James, The Apocryphal New Testament, Oxford: 1955, pp. 181-193.

Bousset, Antichrist
     W. Bousset, The Antichrist Legend, tr. A.H.
     Keane, London: Hutchinson, 1896.

British Library Catalogue
     F.C. Conybeare, Catalogue of the Armenian Manu-
     scripts in the British Museum, London: British
     Museum, 1913.

Bzommar Catalogue
     M. Keschischian, Katalog der armenischen Hand-
     schriften in der Bibliothek des Klosters Bzommar,
     1-2, Vienna: Mechitarist Press, 1964, 1971
     (Armenian).

Erevan Catalogue
     Ō.Eganyan, A. Zeyt'unyan and P'. Ant'abyan,
     Catalogue of the Manuscripts of the Mastoc'
     Library, 1-2, Erevan: Academy of Sciences, 1965,
     1970 (Armenian).

Even-Shmuel
     Y. Even-Shmuel, Midreshei Geulah, Tel-Aviv:
     Mosad Bialik, 1943 (Hebrew).

Galata Catalogue
     Babken Catholicos, Catalogue of the Manuscripts
     of the Armenian National Library of Galatia,
     Antelias: Catholicossate of Sis, 1961 (Armenian).

Geniza Daniel Apocalypse
     Y. Even-Shmuel, Midreshei Geulah, Tel-Aviv:
     Mosad Bialik, 1943, pp. 249-252.

Heist   W.W. Heist, The Fifteen Signs before Doomsday
     East Lansing: Michigan State College, 1952.

James, Apoc. N.T.
     M.R. James, The Apocryphal New Testament,
     Oxford: 1955.

Jellinek, B.M.
    A. Jellinek, Bet Ha-Midrasch, 1-6, 3ed;
    Jerusalem: Wahrmann, 1967 (Hebrew).

Jerusalem Catalogue
    N. Bogharian, Grand Catalogue of St. James Manu-
    scripts, 1-6, Jerusalem: St. James Press, 1968-
    1976 (Armenian).

Kurdian Catalogue
    Armenian Manuscripts : Catalogue of an Exhibi-
    tion at the University of Kansas Library,
    Kansas: 1955.

Ladder of Jacob
    M.R. James, Lost Apocrypha of the Old Testament,
    London: S.P.C.K., 1920, pp. 96-103.

Last Vision of Daniel
    A. Vassiliev, Anecdota Graeco-Byzantina, 1,
    Moscow: 1893,

New Julfa Catalogue
    S. Ter Avetissian, Katalog der armenischen Hand-
    schriften in der Bibliothek des Klosters in Neu-
    Djoulfa, Vienna: Mechitarist Press, 1970
    (Armenian).

P.G.   J. Migne (ed.) Patrologia Graeca, 1-161, Paris:
          Migne, 1844-1902.

P.L.   J. Migne (ed), Patrologia Latina, 1-221, Paris:
          Migne, 1844-1904.

Paris Catalogue
    F. Macler, Catalogue des manuscrits arméniens
    et georgiens de la Bibliothèque Nationale,
    Paris: Bibliotheque Nationale, 1908.

Pauly-Wissowa
    A.F. von Pauly and G. Wissowa, Real-encyclopadie
    der classischen altertums Wissenschaft, 1-24,
    Stuttgart: Metzler, 1893-1963.

Sefer Eliyyahu
>Y. Even-Shmuel, Midreshei Geulah, Tel-Aviv:
>Mosad Bialik, 1943, pp. 41-48.

Seventh Vision of Daniel
>G. Kalemkiar, Die siebente Vision Daniels,
>Vienna: Mechitarist Press, 1892.

Tabriz Catalogue
>H. Adjarian, Katalog der armenischen Hand-
>schriften in Taebriz, Vienna: Mechitarist Press,
>1910 (Armenian).

Vienna Catalogue
>H. Oskian, Katalog der armenischen Handschriften
>in der Mechitaristen-Bibliothek zu Wien, 2,
>Vienna: Mechitarist Press, 1963 (Armenian).

Wutz
>F.X. Wutz, Onomastica Sacra (Texte und Unter-
>suchungen, 41), Leipzig: Hinrichs, 1915.

SIGNS

/	end of line or page in manuscript
	lacuna in manuscript
·	(over letter) partly legible only
. . .	(on line) words lost by the textual tradition
< >	material introduced from another source
⌐ ⌐	uncorrected corruption
{ }	material introduced from a correction or note in the manuscript by a second hand
∿	order of words reversed
+	adds
1°, 2°	(following letter of word) first, second, etc. occurrence of letter in word or word in verse
A^{*}	text as originally written by scribe
A^{o}	text as corrected by original scribe
A^{1}, A^{2}	f rst, second, etc. corrector (not scribe)
A^{c}	corrector other than scribe

OTHER ABBREVIATIONS

above	written above
col(s)	column(s)
cor	corrected, corrector
corr.for	corrupt for
dittog	dittography
eras	erasure, erased
f., ff.	following
fol(s)	folio(s)
haplgr	haplography
hmarkt	homoeoarchton
hmt	homoeoteleuton
illeg	illegible
inc	beginning
ln(s)	line(s)
let	letter
marg	margin
MS	manuscript
n	note
om	omit
omn	all witnesses
r	recto
rel	all witnesses except those cited by siglum
rep.	reprint
s.v.	(in Index to Onomastica) spelling variant
tantum	only as much text in this unit survives as is cited
tot	totally
v	verso
V(L)L	variant reading(s)
vs(s)	verse(s)

All further abbreviations follow the list in <u>JBL</u> 95 (1976) 334-346.

PART ONE

THE SIGNS OF THE JUDGEMENT

Introductory Remarks

The text which we have entitled The Signs of the
Judgement is extant in very numerous versions in European languages.[1] The Armenian versions were first
printed a few years ago, but their relationship to the
widespread medieval European texts has not been recognized nor have they been translated into any modern
language. The Armenian texts are unique in that they
are the first oriental version of this material known.
In an appendix, a Hebrew version of the work is published here for the first time, together with some
critical comments.

The Manuscripts and Editions

The Armenian version was published in two diploma-
tic printings in 1972 by Bishop Norair Bogharian in his
Grand Catalogue of St. James Manuscripts. These two
texts were based on manuscripts in Jerusalem, so
designated below:

I   Jerusalem, No. 1729, Miscellany copied in the
    monastery of Lim in 1741 C.E., p. 320 (Jerusalem
    Catalogue, 6.40-42);

II Jerusalem, No. 1861, Miscellany copied in New
    Julfa (Isfahan) in 1669 C.E., p. 135 (Jerusalem
    Catalogue, 6.248-254).

These two texts are printed and translated synop-
tically, and the material in which they differ from one
another is italicized.

For the sake of comparison, two Latin versions are
presented: B-that attributed (falsely) to the Venerable
Bede, probably stemming from the eleventh or twelfth
century (Patrologia Latina 94.555):[2] and C - that included in the Historia Scholastica of Peter Comestor

(d. 1179 C.E.; Patrologia Latina 198.1611). A third,
associated Latin version, the oldest form of which
occurs in Peter Damien's De novissimis et Antichristo
(Patrologia Latina 145.840-842) is less closely related
to these two texts and not given here in full.

The Hebrew version occurs in the unique manuscript
of the Chronicle of Jeraḥmeel which is preserved in the
Bodleian Library in Oxford.[3] The manuscript is Bodleian
MS Hebrew d.11, copied by R. Eleazar b. Asher haLevi in
the fourteenth century in the Rhineland.[4] The text
occurs on fols. 257r - 257v. The last third of the
preceding page has been left blank and the text is
provided with its own title which states that it was
drawn from the Book of Jeraḥmeel. It is followed by
a Hebrew translation of Pseudo-Philo, Liber Antiquita-
tum Biblicarum10:3 ff. This material is integrated into
the end of the text of The Signs of the Judgement and,
as it stands, forms a natural continuation of it. The
ink of the manuscript is rubbed at a number of places
on fol. 257r, but all the readings are certain, based
on autopsy examination.

Versions in European Languages

In his study of the legend of The Fifteen Signs of
the Doomsday, W. W. Heist reached certain conclusions
about the origins and growth of this material. Drawing
upon the various versions of the Apocalypse of Thomas,
its earliest form is that found in the Old Irish Saltair
na Rann (tenth century) with another Old Irish work of
the same date, The Evernew Tongue, being a separate,
less important source.[5] The seven subsequent types and
further subtypes which Heist discerns among the more
than eighty versions of this material which he examined
are naturally complex in their composition. A number of
them, including those of pseudo-Bede, Comestor, and
Damien know the attribution to Jerome who supposedly

drew upon Annales Hebraeorum (p. 196).

Furthermore, by his analysis, Heist discovers that additional native Irish versions existed, close to but independent of pseudo-Bede.[6] This, he argues, suggests[7] that the origin of The Signs is to be sought in Ireland, and that this material probably reached its present state in the eleventh or twelfth century.

The Armenian version clearly belongs to the same branch of the stemma as pseudo-Bede, Comestor and Damien, but it is not identical with any single one of them. The meaning of the existence of this version is explored below; it may conceivably indicate that, in spite of Heist's analysis, an earlier stage of this text should be posited. The position of the Hebrew version among the medieval European language witnesses is unclear. It is indubitably of a different type to the Armenian version and to those Latin texts here considered, even though it is a translation from Latin.

The origins of the various separate signs in earlier sources are dealt with very briefly by Heist, passim. In the Commentary we have been concerned chiefly with problems of the Armenian version but, in order to indicate the broad spectrum of sources which The Signs and its immediate ancestors are utilizing, chief parallels in ancient sources are noted.

The Character and Relationships of the
Armenian and Hebrew Versions

The Armenian version is written in good classical Armenian. In II a number of Christian elements may be observed, notably in the framework within which the text is presented. All of these are missing from I.[8] Moreover, the formulation of the conclusion in II, with its reference to St. Gregory and the Pit, indicates the peculiarly Armenian character of this Christian framework. In contrast, in I the text is attributed to a

Jewish source and the significance of this will be
discussed below. Although in I the order of Days XIV
and XV has been reversed, in general this recension
finds corroboration in pseudo-Bede and Comestor in
those cases in which it differs from II. Furthermore,
certain indications of a grammatical type show that
recension II is later in language than recension I.
It is also longer in some places and varies in others.
At one point where II has a lacuna, I preserves the
complete text (Day X).

From a literary examination, the relationship
between the recensions emerges more clearly. It seems
likely that I is more original, for no reason can be
imagined for the rejection of the framework (i.e., the
superscription and the conclusion) of II and its replace-
ment with that of I. On the other hand, reverence for
a national saint does provide an easily understood
motive, so the peculiarly Armenian character of the
framework of II is a clear indication of its secondary
character. Moreover, the framework of recension II
invokes scriptural authority for the signs, yet in the
list of signs itself no verses are alluded to. That
such could have been found is clear from the Latin text
of Peter Comestor who cites verses in his concluding
observations, as well as from the biblicizing recension
of the Hebrew version. This is another indication of
the secondary character of the framework.

In the Table below, the relationship between I, II,
B, and C emerges. First, Armenian and Latin B C represent two independent but closely related forms of the
textual tradition of The Signs. There are numerous cases
in which I and II agree against the reading of B and C.
Some of these are: Superscription, both Latin versions
are attributed to Jerome; Day I, both Armenian versions
add that the purpose of the flood is to show that God
can destroy the earth; Day IX, (Day XIII of B), the

the bones of the dead act in an identical fashion in
both Latin texts, different from Armenian; Day XIII,
(XIV of B), the purpose of the death of all men (so as
to be able to rise in the subsequent resurrection) is
given by Latin, but lacks in both Armenian witnesses.

Second, it may be easily observed from a comparison
of I with II that there are many cases in which II is
longer than I. In virtually none of these cases does
the reading of II find corroboration in Latin B or C.
Such are: Day I, "according to the measure of the
Flood"; Day II, "of the dry land --- be seen"; Day III,
"perish", "sand", "loudly --- stink"; Day IV, "and dry
up"; Day VI, "Mountains and", "with a --- destroyed".
Certain other instances of readings of II against I find
no resolution in Latin B or C. In no case is a clear
agreement between II and Latin B or C against the reading of I to be observed. A marginal exception is Day
III "pisces et" B II; omit C I. This reading is also
conflationary with those listed above.

Third, in Latin B a measure of dislocation of the
order of the text has taken place, particularly the
omission from it of the text of Day XV found in the
other versions. This may be a result of a textual
process (perhaps homoeoteleuton novissima --- nova).

In spite of that, the actual text of B, where it is
extant, has many readings in common with Armenian,
against the readings of C. Such are: Day I, "in loco
suo" C (omit B I II); Day II, "ad ima" B I II (omit C);
Day V "omnes" B I II (omit C); Day IX, "omnes--conver-
tentur" B I II ("aequabitur terra" C); Day XII "de caelo"
B I II (omit C); Day XIII, "omnes homines" B I II
("viventes" C). This indicates that, although the
order of events in B is secondary, its text is important.

Fourth, there are a number of instances in which C
agrees with Armenian, against the reading of B. Such are:

Day VI, "collidentur" C I II ("debellabunt" B); "et unaquaeque"-- fin B (omit C I II); Day VII, "mare" C I II (omit B), "ab ortu --- occasum" B (omit C I II); Day VIII "generalis" C I II ("qualis --- mundi" B); Day IX, "et erit --- terrae" B (omit C I II). From these last two groups of examples it follows that neither B nor C shows a special relationship to Armenian.

TABLE

	Armenian		Latin	
Day	I	II	B	C
I	Flood of 40 cubits, like a wall to show that God can destroy the earth		Flood of 40 cubits like a wall	Flood of 40 cubits like a wall
II	Sea dries up to the depths, scarcely seen	Sea dries up to depths of dry land and water not seen	Sea descends to depths whose summit is scarcely to be seen	Sea descends so as to be just seen
			III They will be in balance as originally	
III	Whales upon water cry out to heaven	Fish and whales upon sand perish, cry out, smell	IV Fish and marine beasts upon water cry out, meaning known only to God	Marine beast upon seas cry out to heaven
			V Waters burn to west (see Arm VII)	
IV	Plants and shoots drip bloody dew	Trees and all plants drip bloody dew and wither up	VI All plants and trees give bloody dew	Sea and waters burn
V	All buildings destroyed		VII All buildings destroyed	Plants and trees give bloody dew

Day	Armenian		Latin	
	I	II	B	C
VI	Rocks smite one another	Mountains and rocks smite one another with a terrible noise and are destroyed	VIII Rocks fight one another, are divided into three parts and each smites the other	Buildings destroyed
VII	Sea and earth are burnt with fire (see B V)			Rocks smite one another
VIII	General earthquake		IX Earthquake un- paralleled since creation	General earthquake
IX	Levelling of mountains and valleys		X All hills and valleys become plain	Levelling of earth
X	Men in caverns come forth, are as mad, unable to talk to each other	Men [lacuna]	XI Men come forth from caverns, run as mad, unable to reply to one another	Men come forth from caves, go as mad, unable to talk to one another
XI	Dead go out of graves	Dead fall out of graves	(See XIII below)	Bones of dead rise and stand on graves
XII	Stars appear to fall from heaven		Stars and signs fall from heaven	Stars fall
			XIII Bones of dead gathered and rise up to graves (see rel.XI)	

Armenian
Latin

Day	I	II	B	C
XIII	All men die		XIV All men die so as to rise with the dead	All men die so as to rise with the dead
XIV	XV Heavens and earth burn	Heavens and earth burn	XV Heavens and earth burn up to the end of hell	Heaven and earth burn
XV	XIV New heavens and earth	New heavens and earth		New heavens and earth

The Hebrew version which has not been included in
the above comparison, is a representative of a text type
showing characteristics independent of both the Latin
and the Armenian texts. It contains an extensive introduction and a long conclusion not found elsewhere. Certain of the signs are quite different (e.g., Day VI) or
formulated very differently (e.g., Day X). Moreover,
the Hebrew version is characterized by a biblicizing
tendency. In numerous cases it has introduced a clear
biblical reference either by reformulation or by addition. It may be of interest to observe that the following chief biblical references are made: 2 Sam 22:8
(Day VIII); Ezek 38:20 (Day IX) Isa 2:19,21 (Day X);
Jer 22:19 (Day XI); Isa 51:6, 34:4 (Day XII);Dan 12:3
(Day XIII). Of these, only the reference in Day X is
to be discerned clearly in the Armenian and Latin B C
versions. In the introductory paragraphs Isa 46:16 is
quoted. In the text of Day XV which is integrated into
the following conclusion, four quotations are strung
together: Dan 12:2-3, Judg 5:31, Isa 52:8, and Joel
4:12.

     This version was apparently translated into Hebrew
from a classical language, probably Latin. This is indicated by the following considerations: First, the
introduction contains a classical (or rather a late
classical) legend about Mt. Olympus and the calculation
of the Olympiads. This legend has a tenuous connection
with the text as it is now preserved, being tied in by
the common interest in the highest mountain. The sentence at the actual point of juncture is incomplete,
which perhaps accounts for this apparent tenuousness.
Yet its very inclusion clearly indicates the character
of the Vorlage of the Hebrew version. The tradition
that Mount Olympus is higher than any other mountain
and therefore is not afflicted by the winds is to be

found in the writings of Isidore of Seville. He states: mons Olympus in ea est qui excellenti vertice tantus adtollitur ut in cacumine eius nec nubes nec venti sentiantur (Etymolog. XIV.4.13).[9] No clear parallel to the part of the story here which speaks of the writing of the names of the Olympic victors in the soft earth at the peak of Mt. Olympus has been found, but there seems to be no reason to doubt its Greek or Latin origins.

Second, the fact that this text is bound together with the translation from Pseudo-Philo which follows it, is indicative, but of course not conclusive of this origin. Third, the text of The Signs of the Judgement contains a transliterated Latin word, balaenas (Day III). Incidentally, this is not the word found in the corresponding place in B and C. This is not surprising for the Latin recension behind the Hebrew version was very different from these texts. From the above considerations, however, it may firmly be concluded that this version was translated into Hebrew from Latin.

This indicates that this Hebrew version cannot be a form of some original from which the extant Latin and Armenian versions were made. Such importance as it has lies in the fact that it is a translation of a Latin text of a type different from B and C. It seems difficult to determine whether the biblicizing reworking was the handiwork of the translator, who incidentally wrote a very literate and pleasing Hebrew, or of the Latin version which he was rendering.

Attribution to a Jewish Source

Armenian I and both Latin versions are attributed to a Jewish original. The Christianization of Armenian II, as indicated above, is specifically Armenian in character and is limited to the framework, not penetrating to the body of the text of The Signs proper. [10]

A title similar to that of I may be observed at the
head of an Armenian text which turns out to be an
extract from the Babylonian Talmud. The exact formulation of that superscription is Եբրայեցի Գրոցն գտաք
"We have found in Hebrew books."[11] This parallel lends
a certain prima facie credibility to the statement made
by I, since it shows that translations of Jewish books
were preserved in Armenian and were provided with accu-
rate attribution.[12] Both Latin texts state that the
work is found in annalibus Hebraeorum which shows a
tradition identical with Armenian.

If, however, the thesis of Heist as to the deriva-
tion of this text from a body of material combining
tenth century Old Irish writings and forms of the Latin
version of the Apocalypse of Thomas is correct, then the
origins of the attribution to Jerome as well as to the
Annales Hebraeorum remain puzzling, as he observes. [13]
This mention of the Annales Hebraeorum may explain the
attribution to the famed Hebraist - Jerome, but why the
work, if it was composed in Ireland in the eleventh
century, should be given a fictitious Jewish source is
obscure.

The question of the original language of the Armenian version remains without solution. It is improbable
that Armenian is original, although doubtless the framework of II was composed in Armenian. Whether its original was Latin or Greek or another language cannot be
determined on any objective grounds that could be
discerned by the present writer. Heist's theories
would demand an eleventh century date at the earliest,
and presumably a Latin Vorlage.

Although it thus seems likely that the document is
of Christian origin, it remains notable that the text
itself contains no clearly Christian elements, nor is
any of the portents listed necessarily drawn from the
New Testament. Admittedly, some of them are paralleled

in later Christian sources alone but granted the highly
conservative, traditional nature of these signs, indeed
of much of what is contained in the literature on these
and related topics, as well as the possibility or even
probability of mutual influence, it will readily be
conceded that the Christian character of a single sign
or of the pattern of occurrence of a number of signs
must be very distinctive indeed to serve as sole and
conclusive proof of a Christian origin.[14] Mere occurrence in a Christian apocalypse is not enough.

The discovery of an Armenian version which has
undergone certain textual development in that language
may serve to open up the issue of origins once more.
It could, of course, be a translation from Latin,
depending ultimately on Old Irish sources. Perhaps,
however, the filiation suggested by Heist should take
clearer account of the possible origins of a list of
fifteen signs in older writings, parallel to his suggested Irish source documents. This would not be out
of keeping with the unique role of Ireland in preserv-
ing ancient texts little known elsewhere in Europe.[15]

The Character of the Document

The text is a schematic enumeration of the signs
and portents which are to occur during a period of fifteen days preceding the Last Judgement. The idea that
various upheavals of nature and its order are to precede
the eschaton is an ancient one indeed. It may already
be observed in the Jewish literature of the period of
the Second Temple, which in its turn draws upon more
antique sources in the Bible.[16] One of the salient
points in which The Signs of the Judgement appears
to be unusual when compared with the sources of that
era is in the precise distribution of these events over
a designated period of fifteen days.

The idea that these portents, the "Messianic Woes" as they may be called, were divided into parts is to be found in 2 Apoc. Bar. 27 which refers to twelve parts. This text, stemming from a work composed soon after the end of the first century C.E., is very like another document, a Baraitha which has been preserved in the Babylonian Talmud, Sanhedrin, fol. 97a. In this, a week of years at the close of which the Messiah will come is described and the events which will take place in each year adnumbrated. In both of these documents, the actual events which will take place in each "part" or "year" bear little resemblance to those in The Signs.[17]

An even closer parallel to our text is to be found in The Apocalypse of Thomas suggested by Heist to be an indirect source of The Signs. Here a week of days is delineated, which are "the seven signs (before) the ending of the world".[18] The events of each day are set forth, attributed to a given hour of the day.[19]

As in the two cases mentioned in the last paragraph the actual events, except for one or two very commonplace features, like earthquake, are very little like those of The Signs. The Apocalypse of Thomas is fairly ancient, being extant in a fifth-century fragment. In it, the week of days is mentioned, a measure of time standing in obvious relationship to the week of years in Sanhedrin, fol. 97a and in contrast with the fifteen days here.[20]

Structurally, in a final parallel to be noted, the strict timetable for the whole eschatological process, particularly in its more cataclysmic aspects, is to be observed in Sefer Eliyyahu. Due to the corruption of the dates in the extant manuscripts, it is quite difficult to discern the actual scheme of the chronology.[21]

The Signs appears to be rather inconsequent and to be composed of a series of traditional signs and portents and groups of such. Yet the relationship between

the individual signs and groups of signs has not been
adjusted or adapted to an overall conceptual structure.
This is a common literary feature of both Jewish and
Christian apocalypses, particularly of the later ones,
often a result of heavy dependence on earlier written
and oral sources.

The teaching of the document is typical of a pattern of apocalyptic eschatology which foresaw an increase of chaos and disorder in the world, presaging
the coming of the eschaton. In very many of the texts,
the chaos and disorder lead to or stem from the break-
down of the structure of human society.[22] In The Signs
of the Judgement the scope of the vision is cosmic; the
order of the cosmos will collapse and the sea, the earth,
the mountains, indeed the whole world will be subject to
a series of cataclysms. Consequently, the resolution
and renewal which are to follow the chaos will also be
of cosmic proportions.

The contrast of two ages is implied by this; the
time before the end is divided into fifteen measured
days which can be predicted in advance. The Signs of
the Judgement is thus based upon a view which teaches
a division of the times by a predetermined plan. The
predictions make quite explicit the very day upon which
each portent will happen. A somewhat similar chronological precision of predictions is to be observed in
the Baraitha in b. Sanhedrin fol. 97a. Like The Signs
of the Judgement that text discusses the actual units of
time. In the similar passage in 2 Apoc. Bar. 27, the
parts into which the events are divided are the subject
of discussion, not the exact days or years upon which
they will take place. The view expressed by the Baraitha in Sanhedrin, The Signs of the Judgement, and
Sefer Eliyyahu implies an extreme degree of historical
determinism.

It is appropriate to mention a few other peculiar-
ities of this text. The first is the very number fifteen, for which no rationale at all is apparent. This
contrasts with the Baraitha and the Apocalypse of Thomas
which have "a week" (i.e., of years) and highlights the
author's determinism as well as the vividness of his
imagination. Second, strangely, the text preserves no
hint of belief in an Anti-Christ or an Anti-Messiah such
as Armillos. This is a feature common to many of the
later apocalypses which the commentary shows to have
much in common with The Signs of the Judgement. Finally,
the text mentions no messiah or savior and no angels;
no cosmic or super-human protagonists figure in the
events. "Mythical" or "semi-mythical" features such
as frequently characterize the apocalypses, particularly
the later ones, are absent from this work.

Some remarks may be added on its place within the
Armenian tradition. The Armenians were rather interest-
ed in works of an apocalyptic character, often of the
type of those compositions of the Byzantine period which
were characterized by a wealth of circumstantial prediction, usually political in character. This is witnessed
by the abundance of such material composed or transmit-
ted in the Armenian language, including such writings as
The Seventh Vision of Daniel, The Vision of Enoch, The
Vision of Sahak, the Armenian additions to 4 Ezra and
a number of other works. A text like The Signs of the
Judgement doubtless seemed important to scribes and
thinkers preoccupied with this kind of speculation. It
would not be surprising to find that it, in its turn,
served as a source for some medieval Armenian apocalyp-
ticist.

1. Heist 23-34 outlines the material. He consulted
   eighty-nine versions of the legend, see pp. 204-
   212 for details. See also M. McNamara, The Apocrypha in the Irish Church (Dublin: Dublin Insti-
   tute Advanced Study, 1975) 128-132.

2. See Heist 96-7.

3. The existence of this version was brought to my
   attention by David Flusser who also kindly discussed it with me and made invaluable suggestions
   as to some of the readings and their interpretations.
   Part of the Chronicle of Jerahmeel was published in
   English translation by Moses Gaster, The Chronicles
   of Jerahmeel Or, The Hebrew Bible Historiale (London
   Royal Asiatic Society, 1899). The sections of the
   manuscript parallel to Pseudo-Philo, Liber Antiqui-
   tatum Biblicarum have been published by Daniel J.
   Harrington in Hebrew with a parallel English translation in The Hebrew Fragments of Pseudo-Philo
   (Texts and Translations 3; Pseudepigrapha Series 3;
   Missoula: SBL, 1974). His text does not contain the
   Hebrew version of the section of Bib. Ant. 10:3f.
   which follows The Signs of the Judgement in the
   manuscript as noted below.

4. On the manuscript see: A. Neubauer and A.E. Cowley,
   Catalogue of Hebrew Manuscripts in the Bodleian Lib-
   rary (Oxford: 1906) 2. cols. 209-215, esp. col. 213
   (MS No. 2797),

5. Heist passim and see conclusions, 193-195.

6. Ibid. 197-198.

7. Ibid. 195.

8. See in detail in the commentary on the superscription
   and the conclusion below.

9. The absence of meteorological phenomena on Mt. Olympus and the special quality of the air upon it are
   already noted in Odyssey VI, 41-45. That this is a
   function of its height is also the view of Augustine,
   Civ. Dei XV, 27. See in detail also: Pauly-Wissowa,

18, 1. 308-309.

10. See below, commentary on the superscription.

11. See: Michael E. Stone, "An Armenian Translation of a Baraitha in the Babylonian Talmud", HTR 68 (1970) 151-154

12. See also further comments in: Michael E. Stone, "Jewish Literature from the Period of the Second Temple in Armenian Literature", Lectures at the History Research Meetings, (Jerusalem; Israel Historical Society, 1973) 263-5 (Hebrew). This statement does not necessarily imply direct translation from Hebrew into Armenian.

13. Heist 108.

14. On these questions, see also: W. Bousset, Antichrist, passim.

15. Heist 201-202.

16. Convenient lists of sources are to be found in many books dealing with Jewish eschatology in the period of the Second Temple, and these sources will become evident in the course of the discussion of the parallels to the events listed in The Signs. See, by way of example: D. S. Russell, The Method and Message of Jewish Apocalyptic (Philadelphia: Fortress, 1964) 271-276 and the sources and bibliography there.

17. A comparison of the Baraitha and 2 Apoc. Bar. 27 may be found in: E.E. Urbach, The Sages: Their Concepts and Beliefs, (tr. I Abrahams; Jerusalem; Magnes, 1975) 676-678

18. The English is drawn from: M.R. James , Apoc N.T. 558-62.

19. No rationale seems evident for the choice of hours.

20. On the date of The Apocalypse of Thomas and other critical problems, see: E. Henneke and W. Schneemelcher, New Testament Apocrypha, tr. by R. McL.

Wilson (Philadelphia: Westminster, 1965) 2.798-800.
Further bibliography is to be found there.

21. Compare the textual material presented by M. But-
    tenweiser, Die hebräische Elias-Apokalypse
    (Leipzig: Pfeiffer, 1926) 16-26 and by Even-Shmuel
    39-48, 51-54, 374-379. The timetable of salvifica-
    tory events of Sefer Zerubbabel is also analogous
    to this material, ibid., pp. 71-88, 379-389.

22. The sources are manifold. See, for examples of
    one type of text: 4 Ezra 13:29 ff., Matt 24:7,
    m. Sot. 9:15, 1 Enoch 56:7, Melito, Pasch. Hom.
    51 ff., et al.

Եւ այլ վարդապետք ասեն
Թէ ընդերցաք ի գիրս Հրէից
որ լինելոց են ժէ նշան,
ի ժէ աւուրս յառաջ քան
զդատաստանն:

վասն զալստեան Որդոյն
Աստուծոյ եւ կատարածի
աշխարհի, թէ որպէս է
անեղ դատաստանն: Արդ մեք
որ ակն ունիմք զալստեանն
Քրիստոսի Աստուծոյ մերոյ,
վկայութեամբ Սուրբ Գրոց
եւ բանիւ առաքելոց եւ
մարգարէից եւ վկայութեամբ
Սուրբ Աւետարանին
Քրիստոսի որ այսպէս
լինելոց է աւերումն
աշխարհի ի վերջին ժամանակն,
ժէ նշան լինի յառաջ քան
զգալուստն Քրիստոսի.

I

And other doctors say, "We
have read in the books of
the Jews that there are going to be fifteen signs on
fifteen days before the
Judgement.

II

Concerning the coming of
the Son of God and the end
of the world, or in what
fashion is the terrible
Judgement. Now, we who
hope for the coming of
Christ our God, by the
witness of the Sacred
Scriptures, and by the
word of Apostles and
Prophets, and by the
witness of the holy
Gospel of Christ, (know)
that in this fashion is
the destruction of the
world going to be at the
last time. There are
fifteen signs before the
coming of Christ.

I   Առաջին օրն բարձրացի ծովն Խ կանգուն ի վերայ

      բարձրագոյն *լերանց*   *լերանց ըստ չափոյ*

                               ջրհեղեղին

      եւ կացցէ իբրեւ պարիսպ (զպարիսպ II) շուրջ զաշխարհաւս

      ի *նշան* թէ կարող է   զի տեսցեն եւ զարմասցին

      Աստուած *տապալել* զաշ-   եւ զիտասցեն թէ կարող է

      խարհ *որպէս* *հեղեղաւ*։   Աստուած *ջրհեղեղաւ*

                                անցուցանել զաշխարհս։

II   Երկրորդ օրն իջցէ ծովն ի խոնարհ

      մինչ *հազիւ* երեւեսցի։   գամբի եւ այլ ո*չ*

                               երեւի *ջուր*։

III   Երրորդ օրն կէտք մեծա-   Երրորդ օրն ձկունք եւ

      մեծք ելեալ ի վերայ   կէտք մեծամեծք ելեալ

      երեսաց *ջրոց* գոչես-   տապալեն ի վերայ աւագոյ

      ցեն *մինչեւ* *լերկինս*։   մեծամայն գոչեսցեն

                                եւ մեռանեն եւ *նեխեալ*

                                հոտեցնեն զաշխարհս։

IV   Չորրորդ օրն տունկք   Չորրորդ օրն *ծառք* եւ

      եւ բոյսք կաթեցու-   տունկք եւ *ամենայն* բոյսք

      ցանեն գող արեան։   գող արեան կաթեցնեն *եւ*

                                չորանան։

V   Հինգերորդ օրն կործանեցին (կործանին II) ամենայն

      շինուածք։

I On the first day the sea will rise forty cubits above

the highest mountains   the mountains according to

the measure of the Flood

and it will stand like a wall around the world

as a sign that God is   that they might see and

able to destroy the earth   wonder and know that God

as by a flood.   is able to make this earth

pass away through a flood.

II On the second day the sea will go down to a depth

until it will be seen   of the dry land and no

with difficulty   more water will be seen.

III On the third day, very   On the third day, very

great whales, having   great fish and whales

come forth upon the   having come forth, perish

face of the waters, will   upon the sand. They will

cry up to the heavens.   cry loudly and die and,

having rotted will make

this world stink.

IV On the fourth day   On the fourth day trees

plants and shoots shall   and plants and all shoots

drip dew of blood.   shall drip dew of blood

and dry up.

V On the fifth day all buildings shall be (are II)

destroyed.

VI   *Վեցերորդ օրն վէմք*   *Վեցերորդ օրն _լերինք_ եւ*
      հարկանիցեն ընդ   *վէմք հարկանեն ընդ*
      իրեարս: *իրարս _աՀագին_ _թնդմամբ_*
                                    _եւ_ _բլին_:

VII   *Եօթներորդ օրն ծով եւ երկիր վառեցին Հրով:*

VIII *Ութերորդ օրն եղիցի ընդՀանուր (ընթՀանուր II) գետ-*
      նաշարժ:

IX   *Իններորդ օրն ամենայն լերինք եւ ձորք Հաւասարեցին*
      (Հաւասարեցեն II):

X   *Տասներորդ օրն, եւեաւ մարդիկ[23] որ լինին ի յայրս*
      եւ ի խորշս երկրի, եւ շրջեցին որպէս խելագարեալս,
      եւ ոչ կարասցեն խօսել ընդ միմեանս:

XI   *Մետասաներորդ օրն ամե-*   *Մետասաներրորդ օրն ամե-*
      նայն _մեռեալք_ արտաքս   *նայն _մեռելնին_ արտաքս*
      գնան ի գերեզմանաց   *ի գերեզմանաց իւրեանց*
      իւրեանց: *անկանին:*

XII   *Երկոտասաներորդ օրն*   *Երկոտասաներորդ օրն*
      *_թուեցին_ աստեղաց _թէ_*   *_թուեցեն_ աստեղաց*
      անկեաւ յերկնից: *_անկանել_ յերկնից:*

XIII *Երեքտասաներորդ օրն մեռանիցին (մեռանիցեն II) ամենայն*
      մարդիկ:

VI On the sixth day rocks   On the sixth day mountains
    shall be smitten against   and rocks smite against
    one another.   one another with a fear-
                                full thundering and are
                                destroyed.

VII On the seventh day the sea and the earth will be
     burnt with fire.

VIII On the eighth day there will be a general earth-
      quake.

IX On the ninth day all mountains and valleys will be
    leveled.

X On the tenth day, men [23] who are in the caves and
   caverns (or: holes) of the ground having come forth,
   they will go around like madmen and will be unable
   to speak with one another.

XI On the eleventh day all   On the eleventh day all
    the dead come outside   die. They fall outside
    their graves.   their graves.

XII On the twelfth day stars   On the twelfth day stars
     shall appear to have   shall appear
     fallen from heaven.   to fall from heaven.

XIII On the thirteenth day, all men shall die.

23 II omits the text from Վարդիկ to the end of the
    tenth day.

XV Հնգետասաներորդ օրն   XIV Չորեքտասաներորդ օրն
    վառեցին երկինք եւ   վառեց ն երկինք եւ
    երկիր, այսինքն   երկիր որպէս
    օդ: օդ:

XIV Չորեքտասաներորդ օրն   XV Հնգետասաներորդ օրն
    եղիցի երկինք եւ   եղիցի երկին եւ
    երկիր նոր.   երկիր նոր:
    եւ յարիցեն ամենայն   Յայնժամ Գաբրիէլ հրեշ-
    մեռեալք: տակապետն հրամանաւ

                               Աստուծոյ գոչէ զձայն

փողոյն ի վերայ Վիրապի մեր Լուսաւորչին, թէ աւա
Քրիստոս գա, արիք ընդ առաջ նորա. յայնժամ յառնեն
սուրբքն:

XV   On the <u>fifteenth</u> day   XIV   On the <u>fourteenth </u>day

the heavens and the   the heavens and earth

earth shall be burnt,   shall be burnt <u>like</u>

<u>that</u> <u>is</u> <u>to</u> <u>say</u> the   atmosphere.

atmosphere.

XIV On the <u>fourteenth</u> day   XV   On the <u>fifteenth</u> day

there will be a new   there will be a new

heaven and earth,   heaven and earth.

and all the dead shall   Then Gabriel, the

rise.   archangel, by God's

command sounds the

blast of the trumpet

over the Pit of our Illuminator, 'Behold, Christ

is coming, rise up before him.' Then the saints

arise.

De XV Signis

B	C
De Quindecim Signis	De Signis Quindecim dierum ante judicium
Quindecim signa quindecim dierum ante diem judicii, invenit Hieronymus in annalibus Hebraeorum.	Hieronymus autem in annalibus Hebraeorum invenit signa quindecim dierum ante diem judicii, sed utrum continui futuri sint dies illi, an interpolatim, non expressit.
I. Prima die eriget se mare in altum quadraginta cubitis, super altitudines montium, et erit quasi murus, et amnes similiter.	Prima die eriget se mare quadraginta cubitis super altitudinem montium stans in loco suo quasi murus.
II Secunda die descendent usque ad ima, ita ut summitas eorum vix conspici possit.	Secunda tantum descendet, ut vix posset videri.
III Tertia die erunt in aequalitate, sicut ab exordio.	Tertia marinae belluae apparentes super mare,

dabent rugitus usque ad

coelum;

IV Quarta die pisces et   quarta ardebit mare,

omnae belluae marinae,   et aquae;

et congregabuntur super

aquas, et dabunt voces

et gemitus, quarum

significationem nemo

scit nisi Deus.

V Quinta die ardebunt ipsae   quinta herbae et arbores

aquae ab ortu suo usque   dabunt rorem sanguinem;

ad occasum.

VI Sexta die omnes herbae,   Sexta ruent aedificia;

et arbores sanguineum

rorem dabunt.

VII Septima die omnia aedifi-   septima petrae ad invicem

ca destruentur.   collidentur;

VIII Octava die debellabunt   octava fiet generalis

petrae ad invicem, et   terrae motus;

unaquaeque in tres partes

se dividet, et unaquaeque

pars collidet adversus

alteram.

IX Nona die erit terrae   nona aequabitur terra;
    motus qualis non fuit
    ab initio mundi.

 X Decima die omnes colles   decima exibunt homines de
    et valles in platitudinem   cavernis, et ibunt velut
    convertentur, et erit   amentes, nec potuerunt
    aequalitas terrae.   mutuo loqui.

XI Undecima die homines   undecima surgent ossa
    exibunt de cavernis   mortuorum, et stabunt
    suis, et current quasi   super sepulcra;
    amentes, nec poterit
    alter respondere alteri.

XII Duodecima die cadent   duodecima cadent
    stellae et signa de   stellae;
    coelo.

XIII Decima tertia de congre-   tredecima morientur
     gabuntur ossa defuncto-   viventes, ut cum mortuis
     rum, et exsurgent usque   resurgent;
     ad sepulcrum.

XIV Decima quarta die omnes   quartadecima ardebit
    homines morientur, ut   caelum, et terra;
    simul resurgant cum
    mortuis.

XV. Decima quinta die ardebit   quintadecima fiet

    terra usque ad inferni   coelum novum, et terra

    novissima, et post erit   nova, et resurgent

    dies iudicii.   omnes.

C continues:

Et addidit Jesus: "Sicut fulgur exit ab oriente et
paret usque in occidentem, sic erit adventus Filii
hominis (Matt 24:27, cf. Luke 27:24)," subitus scilicet,
et coruscus, et tunc apparebit signum Filii hominis in
coelo, id est in aere, supra locum unde ascendit, et
ante eum erunt instrumenta mortis suae, quasi vexilla
triumphi, crux, clavi, lancea, et in carne ejus vide-
buntur cicatrices, ut videant in quem pupugerunt
(Rev 1:7), et in valle Josephat judicabitur omnis homo,
angelis congregantibus eos (Mark 12:27).
*Additio 1. Nota quod dicitur judicium futurum in vale
Josephat. Sed nota quod tunc non erit vallis, quia
quarto decimo die aequabitur terra, sed contra illum
locum erit. Vel propter interpretationen hujus nominis
Josephat, interpretatur enim judicium. Vallis ergo
Josephat, humilitatem judicii sonat.

COMMENTARY ON THE ARMENIAN TEXT

<u>Superscription</u>: I clearly lacks all of the Christian
elements which may be discerned in II. The last sentence in II, "There are fifteen signs before the coming
of Christ" is exactly parallel in function to the latter
part of the sentence in I. The preceding material in II
refers to the witness of the Sacred Scripture, of Apostles, and of prophets to the destruction of the world
as described in the following. This is, in our view, an
expansion, since there is no further reference to any
scriptural verse or proof text throughout all of the
following Armenian document. In principle, it would
seem unlikely that I was derived from II, while II might
represent an "Armenization" of a text like I (See also
Introductory Remarks above).

<u>Day I</u>: The variation between the recensions does not
affect the meaning. The flood referred to is clearly
an eschatological repetition of Noah's flood, as is
indicated by the mention of how high the water rose
above the highest mountains (cf. Gen 7:20). The actual
measure of depth differs, the Bible giving fifteen
cubits, as against our text's forty (see on Hebrew version). The very destruction by flood is strange, in
view of God's covenant with Noah (Gen 9:11, cf. 8:21,22).
Few parallels to this idea can be found in the chief
listings of similar events. The phrase "like a wall" is
reminiscent of Exod 14:22,29 etc.

Ancient parallels: Arm. 4 Ezra 6:20, <u>Seventh
Vision of Daniel</u> p. 42, lns. 15-6.

<u>Day II</u>: The variation between the two Armenian recen-
sions, although substantial from a textual viewpoint,
makes no major difference in meaning.

Ancient parallels: T. Levi 4:1, 4 Ez 6:24, Ap.Elij.
3:63, Ps.-Hippolytus, De consum. mundi 27 (P.G.10.929-932):
cf. As. Mos. 10:6.[24]

Day III: Recension II adds to the contents of I the
idea of the death and putridity of the fish and whales.
In its text for this day, for the first time, two of
those late, post-classical grammatical forms are encountered, which are typical of this text, viz. մեռանեն
and հուրեցնեն.

Ancient parallels: Jub. 23:18, Lactantius, Instit.
VII,16,8; exactly parallel - Ephraem Syrus texts apud
Bousset, Antichrist, pp. 195 ff. Ps. - Hippolytus,
De consum mundi 27 (P.G. 10.929).

Day IV: Here once more, recension II introduces features additional to those found in recension I. "The
trees" are added to the list of flora (cf. Latin B C)
which, as well as dripping blood, also dry and wither.

Ancient parallels: 4 Ezra 5:5, Barn. 12:1, Ladder
of Jacob 7; cf. Sib. Or. 3:684, 804.

Day V: Here the text preserved by the two recensions of
Armenian is identical, except for a minor variation of
verb form.

It is noteworthy that there is a certain irration-
ality running through all of these signs as they are
presented in the text. The very first event adnumbrated,
the flood, is described as being so severe as to reach
a depth of forty cubits and destroy the whole earth. Yet,
plants still exist until Day IV, buildings are only
overthrown on Day V, while the intervening events make

---

24. The ultimate background may lie in the myth that
has also informed passages such as Isa 51 :10 and others
in the Bible. On this see, in general: F.M.Cross Jr.,
"The Divine Warrior in Israel's Early Cult", Biblical
Motifs: Origins and Transformations, ed. A. Altmann,
Cambridge, Mass. Harvard, (1966) 11-30.

the survival of the troglodytes of Day X, or of the "all
men" of Day XIII rather unlikely, to say the least. On
the other hand, occasional groups of two or three days
seem to be held together by a logical or at least a
plausibly coherent structure. Such are Days I, II and
III, which move from flood, through drying up of the
sea, to the death of maritime creatures and see further
observations on these, below. The same seems to be
true of Days VIII and IX and Days XIV and XV. There is,
however, no embracing concept, such as a movement from
a lesser to a more general measure of destruction, which
controls the overall ordering of the signs. Furthermore, either Day VII or Day XIV seems to be redundant,
and other equally anomalous features may be observed.

     Ancient Parallels: _Apocalypse of Thomas_, 5b6-7.

Day VI: Again, recension II adds certain elements
absent from I, notably the thundering of the rocks and
their destruction. The verb ﬔﬔﬔ "destroyed" is
written with a   ﬔ   "b" instead of the correct ﬔ
"p". This makes it likely that the scribe responsible
for this error spoke a dialect in which   ﬔ   "b" was
pronounced as "p", as in Modern West Armenian.

     Ancient Parallels: _Sib.Or._3:680-681, _T. Levi_ 4:1,4
Ezra 4:5, _Ap. Elijah_ 3:84, cf. Ezek 38:20, _I Enoch_ 50:
6-7, _As. Mos._ 10:4.

Day VII: According to Latin, only the sea burns at this
point, while all versions have a general conflagration
on Day XIV, q.v. In Armenian, however, a more cosmic
dimension is implied, and so some general parallels may
be included at this point. The idea of a burning of the
world with fire is rather widespread in eschatological
writings.

     Ancient Parallels: fire originates from earth 4
Ezra 5:8; from heavens _Sib.Or._ 2:196-197, 3:542-543,
690, _2 Apoc. Bar._ 27:10. Geniza Daniel Apocalypse, 1n.36,

Seventh <u>Vision of Daniel</u>, p. 42 lns. 16-7, <u>The Last</u>
<u>Vision of Daniel</u>, p. 47; from heaven and earth <u>Ap. Elijah</u>
3:82; general conflagration Josephus <u>Ant</u>. I, 70; Philo,
<u>Vit. Mos</u>. 2:263; <u>Vit. Ad</u>. 49-50; cf. <u>Aqadat Bereshit</u>
(Jellinek, <u>B.M.</u> 4)1; <u>2 Apoc. Bar.</u> 70:8 .[25]

<u>Day VIII</u>: The same underlying dialectical feature, ob-
served in a note on Day VI above, also appears here. The
form ԸՍՔՆԱՆՈՒՐ of II reads Ω "t" for ո "d" which latter was probably pronounced by the scribe as "t".

Ancient parallels: Ezek 38:14, 4 Ezra 6:20, <u>Sib</u>.
<u>Or</u>. 3:675, <u>2 A.Bar</u> 70:8, Matt 24:7, <u>Sefer Eliyahu</u> ln.23
Geniza Daniel Apocalypse, ln. 41 <u>et al</u>.

<u>Day IX:</u> The verb form of II, apparently an active for a
medio-passive, recurs below and is doubtless dialectal.
The levelling of the mountains is probably to be regard-
ed as the outcome of the earthquake.

Ancient parallels: <u>Sib. Or</u>. 8:236, Lacantius, <u>In-</u>
<u>stitut</u>. VII, 16, 11; cf. Isa 40:4 (context differs). [26]

<u>Day X</u>: The idea of men hiding from the fear of God in
caverns and caves is to be found in Isa 2:10, and particularly 19 and 21. It is there used in a context of a

25. This is probably not the "testing" fire referred to
by T. Abr. A,13, Didache 14:5. For a selection of later
sources see: Bousset, <u>Antichrist</u> 238-245. The idea of
the cataclysmic fire is well known in Greek thought. See
e.g., the material cited by J. Burnet, <u>Early Greek Phil-</u>
<u>osophy</u> (rep; London: Black, 1945) 157-160. The sources
are manifold. See also: T.F. Glasson, <u>Greek Influence</u>
<u>in Jewish Eschatology</u>, (London: 1961) 77-80, who
quotes some further details. On this concept in Jewish
sources, see the detailed treatment by L.Ginzberg, "Mab-
bul Shel Esh", <u>Haqoren</u> 8 (5672), 35-51 [in Hebrew].
26. It may be observed that passages relating signs and
portents accompanying theophanies have much in common
with the Messianic signs. <u>Sib. Or</u>.3:683-692, describing
God's warlike theophany has, inter alia, the falling of
walls, flooding by torrents of blood, rocks flowing with
blood, fire, and cataclysms of rain. The investigation
of this subject, however, would be tangential to the aim
of the present study.

prophecy of God's epiphany to exact judgement from the
wicked. The verses in Isaiah combined to produce a clear
picture of men hiding themselves in caverns and clefts
of rocks in order to escape God's judgement. They were
taken up also by Rev 6:15-16, at the opening of the
sixth seal. There seems to be no reason to regard The
Signs as derived from Revelation rather than from Isaiah.
Indeed, there appear to be some indications that the
contrary is the case. Where The Signs is almost literally identical with Isaiah 2:19, "caves...and rocks of
the mountains". The Latin version reads in cavernis,
which is not helpful in making the determination. This
feature is also found in Seventh Vision of Daniel, p.41,
lns. 26-7. The Armenian terms differ from The Signs.
Less similar is Mark 13:14. The balance of the descrip-
tion in The Signs has no parallel elsewhere.[27]

27. It might be maintained that the stars are said to
fall both in Revelation and in The Signs and that this
indicates that The Signs is dependent on Revelation.
Yet, in this latter work, the falling of the stars precedes the incident of the caves and is an integral part
of a list of astronomical portents, none of the others
of which is found in The Signs (except for the commonplace earthquake). In The Signs the falling of the
stars follows the caves and is separated by the distinctive falling of the dead from their tombs. In Latin
B this is not the case, but its order of events is secondary. The falling of the stars is very common in the
lists of the Messianic woes (see below). It seems,
therefore, that no significance should be attached to
the conjunction of these elements. Incidentally, the
falling of the stars also takes its origin in the Book
of Isaiah (34:4). Compare also Otot Hamashiah (Jellinek,
B.M. 3) 50. The caves and caverns occur in a number of
texts as the places to which the righteous flee when the
Antichrist comes. For a selection see: Bousset, 212
ff., cf. Ps. Hippol. De consum mundi 32 (P.G. 10 p.936)
In these texts, on the whole, there is no clear evidence
of dependence on Revelation and it is likely that some
common tradition is here involved, as Bousset, indeed,
suggests.

Day XI: There is no really significant difference between the two recensions. In I, the dead go from their
tombs, while in II, they fall from them. This is a mac-
abre portent and not the issuing forth of the dead for
resurrection. In the Latin versions, the bones of the
dead are gathered together and they rise up in their
tombs. No parallels are known, unless it be the saints
rising from their tombs at the crucifixion, Matt 27:52.
See also Commentary on Hebrew version.

Day XII: There are certain anomalous features in the
language of this sentence. The verb is active in II
instead of the medio-passive of I (see note on Day IX,
above). The variation between the recensions does not
affect the import of the passage.

     Ancient parallels: Matt 24:29, Seventh Vision
of Daniel p. 42, lns. 14-5, Rev 6:13 - all dependent on
Isa 34:4; Sib. Or. 2:202, Lactantius, Institut. VII.16,
8-10, Book of John the Evangelist p. 192, Ps. Hippolytus,
de consum. mundi 37 (P.G. 10:940).

Day XIII: The variant verb form of recension II is identical with that noted above, see notes on Day IX.

Day XIV: In I, fairly obviously, the numbering of the
fourteenth and fifteenth days has been reversed. Recension II, at this point, has preserved the original order.
The idea of the conflagration was discussed above (see
note on Day VII). The burning described in the present
context is apparently of more universal measure than that
of Day VII. The final phrase is unclear in Armenian and
is missing from Latin.

     Ancient parallel: Ps. -Hippolytus, De consum.
mundi 37 (P.G. 10.940).

<u>Day</u> <u>XV</u>: The idea of the new heavens and the new earth is very widespread, and there is no point in documenting it here.

<u>Conclusion</u>: The form of the Conclusion in recension II clearly indicates its Armenian origin. The final phrase of I could be Jewish or Christian, Greek, Latin or Armenian. The blowing of the trumpet here is unlike 4 Ezra 6:23 where it has a different function and meaning, but may be compared with Didache 16:6, <u>Seventh</u> <u>Vision</u> <u>of</u> <u>Daniel</u>, p. 47, <u>Otot</u> <u>Ḥamashiaḥ</u> (Jellinek, <u>B.M.</u>2)61-2 , Lactantius, <u>Institut</u>. VII, 16, 11, and many other sources.

HEBREW VERSION

א 257   חמש עשרה אותות לפני יום הדין

מספר ירחמיאל:

והמים גברו חמש עשרה אמה ממעל

להרים בימי המבול כי כן נתמלאה

כל מחטאת בני האדם וכן יעשה

ליום הדין כאשר נעשה

במבול, כי ביום הדין ישפט הק⟨דוש⟩

את עולמו באש שני כי באש

5   יייי נשפט:/ ויגדל האש

עד חמש עשרה אמה ממעל להר תבור מכל

ההרים הוא הר הנקרא

אולימפוס, כי מאותו הר עשו היונים

את מניין האולימפיאדס, כי לארבעה שנים

היו עולים בהר אולימפוס והיו כותבין

בעפר תיחו⟨ח⟩ אשר על

ההר את נצחונם, ולא היה רוח מנשב עליו

מפני גובהו כי האו⟨יר⟩ לא היה

10   ⟨שולט⟩ עליו וגם עוף השמים/לא

פורח עליו ואיש לא היה עולה עליו

אם לא היה נותן בעין ספוג מלא מים

ונחיריו מפני האויר.

ולפני יום הדין חמשה עשר יום

יהיו מופתים בשמים ובארץ,

257r   Fifteen Signs before the Day of Judgement

from The Book of Jerahmeel

And the waters increased to fifteen cubits above

the mountains in the days of the Flood for thus every-

thing was filled with the sins of men and thus will it

happen on the day of judgement as happened in the

Flood.   For on the day of judgement the Ho⟨ly⟩One will

judge his world as it says, "For by fire will the Lord

5 execute judgement" (Isa 66:16)./ And the fire will in-

crease to fiteen cubits above Mt. Tabor, (and above

the highest) of all mountains, the mountain called

Olympus.   For, from that mountain the Greeks made the

reckoning of the Olympiads.   For, each four years they

would ascend Mount Olympus and they would write their

victories in the dust of the soft ear⟨th⟩ which was on

the mountain.   And the wind did not blow upon it be-

cause of its height for the atm⟨osphere⟩ had no

10 ⟨control⟩ over it.   The birds of the heavens too / do

not flutter over it and people did not ascend it un-

less they placed a sponge soaked with water in their

eye(s) and in their nostrils because of the air.

Fifteen days before the day of judgement there

will be portents in the heavens and on the earth, and

והיתה צרה גדולה אשר לא נהייתה

מהיות גוי על הארץ.

ותרעש הארץ ונמסו ההרים

ושאון ימים יהמיון לפלגים

אשר ישח האדם בפחד לבן

15   כי קרוב יום יייי/על כל

הגוים   הוא יום יייי לא יכילו זעמו

ולא יושע כל בשר

כי אם בתשובת   עזיבת

רשעו וישוב אל יייי.

ואלה האותות חמש עשרה בחמשה עשר יום

כל אחד ואחד ביומו:

I   ביום הראשון יצא הים

מחוק גבולו על כל גדותיו

20   וירבו המים/ממעל להרים הגבוהים ארבעים אמה

ויעמדו כחומה.

II   ביום השיני ישובו ויחרבו

עד למעט.

III   ביום השלישי יתראו התנינים הגדולים

אשר בתוך הים מחוסר המים

והם בַלַיְינָש והם גועים

בקולם עד לשמים.

IV   ביום הרביעי יבשו ויחרבו כל המים שבימים

there will be great distress such as has not been from

the time of existence of nations upon the earth. And

the earth will quake and the mountains will melt and

the tumult of the seas will roar in (its) streams,

which a man shall relate to his son in fear of his

15 heart that the day / of the Lord is close upon all the

nations, that is the day of the Lord which his anger

will not contain and all flesh will not be saved ex-

cept by repentance of (i.e. which is) abandoning its

evil; and he will return to the Lord.

And these are the fifteen signs on fifteen days,

each individual one on its day.

I   On the first day the sea will issue forth from the

limit of its boundary over all its shores and the wat-

20 er will rise to forty cubits / above the high mount-

ains and will stand like a wall.

II   On the second day it will subside and dry up until

(it is) few.

III   On the third day the great sea-monsters which are

in the sea will be visible because of the lack of wat-

ter, and they are the balaenas, and they low with

their voice to the heavens.

IV   On the fourth day all the waters in the seas and

ובאגמים ובנהרות ויצמא

25   ויהמה האדם / וההבהמה והעוף:

V   ביום החמשי יבכו האדם וההבהמה והעוף

למים עד שיטיפו דם מעיניהם

וכל האילנות והדשאים יטיפו דם:

VI   ביום הששי יהיו קולות וברקים

ורעמים ורוחות:

VII   ביום השביעי יכתתו כל האבנים

וימסו:

VIII ביום השמיני תרעש ותגעש הארץ

ומוסדות השמים ירגזון:

30   IX   ביום התשיעי יפלו / הבתים

ויפלו המדרגות ויצעקו העצים

והאבנים כצעקת בני אדם:

X   ביום העשירי יכנסו ויבאו בני האדם בסעיפי

הסלעים ובמחילות עפר

מפני פחד יייי:

XI   ביום אחד עשר ינערו עצמות בני אדם

מקבריהם ויושלכו ויסחבו

על פני חוצות:

XII   ביום שנים עשר יפלו הכוכבים והמאורות

ונגולו   השמים (כ) ספר

35   והארץ / כבגד תבלה

lakes and rivers will become dry and dry up and man,

25 beast, and bird will thirst / and groan.

 V On the fifth day man, beast, and bird will weep

  for water until they drip blood from their eyes and

  all the trees and the grasses will drip blood.

 VI On the sixth day there will be sounds and light-

  ning and thunder and winds.

 VII On the seventh day all the stones will be smashed

  and melt.

 VIII On the eighth day the earth will rock and reel and

  the foundations of the heavens will tremble.

I 30IX On the ninth day / the houses will fall and the

  terraces (or: cliffs) will fall and the trees and

  stones will cry out as a human cry.

 X On the tenth day men will enter into the clefts

  of the cliffs and holes of the ground because of the

  terror of the Lord.

 XI On the eleventh day the bones of men will be

  aroused from their graves and will be cast and dragged

  through the streets.

 XII On the twelfth day the stars and the luminaries

  will fall and the heavens will be rolled up as a book

35 and the earth will wear out / like a garment and the

ויפתחו הקברות ויתקעו

השופרות ורבים יקיצו:

XIII ביום שלשה עשר ימותו

ויגוע כל בשר יחד:

2571 XIV ביום ארבעה/עשר ישרפו שמים וארץ

וימסו מאש הגדולה

ויכלו:

XV   ביום חמשה עש ר יבראון בֹ֯א֯ שמים החדשים

והארץ החדשה ויקיצו

שוכני עפר המשכילים ויזהירו

כזוהר הרקיע

וכצאת השמש בגבורתו

ויקבצו בתוך ירושלים עיר הקודש

ויראו עין בעין

בשוב ה' ציון

5   ויאספו / אל עמק יהושפט

לשפט אותם ואז יבראון כולם

ברוח חדשה ונפש חדשה ובריה חדשה

ויבאו לפני המלך ה':

Vacat 12 let and then continues with Ps. Philo, Bib. Ant. 10:3ff.

4 הק>דוש< הקֹ | 6-7 אולימפוס...אולימפיאדס... אולימפוס

קו מאוזן מעל ל-סמ"ך | 8 תיחו>ח< תיחוה | 9

>שולט< שלולט למ"ד 1°מחוקה בקו | 10 האו>יר< האו |

29 >נגולו< נגואלו | >כ<ספר] הספר |

38 >ה< שמים] שמים

graves will be opened and the trumpets will be

blown and many will awake.

XIII   On the thirteenth day they will die and all

flesh will perish together.

257v XIV   On the four/teenth day heaven and earth will

be burnt and melt in the great fire and be des-

troyed.

XV   On the fifteenth day < the > new heavens and

the new earth will be created * and those wise who

dwell in the dust shall awake and will shine like

the brightness of the firmament (Dan 12:2-3) * and

like the sun as it rises in its might (Jud 5:31).

And they shall be gathered in the midst of the holy

city Jerusalem * and eye to eye they will see the

return of the Lord to Zion (Isa 52:8). And they

5 will be gathered / to the valley of Jehosaphat for

their judgement and then they will all be created

with a new spirit and a new soul and a new crea-

tion and they will come before the king, the Lord.

(Continues L.A.B. 10:3ff.)

COMMENTARY ON THE HEBREW VERSION

Title (line 1): The title clearly indicates the origin
of the fragment in the Book or Chronicles of Jerahmeel.
The rest is obvious and is also similar to the titles of
Latin and Armenian.

Introduction (lines 2-11).

The first point made by the introduction is the typ-
ological relationship between Noah's Flood and the flood
which is expected at the eschaton. Just as Noah's Flood
covered the highest mountains, so will the flood of fire.
This relationship was made explicit also in the descrip-
tion of the flood of water which will take place on Day I
according to the Armenian version. The problems inherent
in it were pointed out in the commentary to that place.
In the Introduction to the Hebrew version here, the measure of fifteen cubits is drawn from Gen 7:20 and is not
brought into agreement with that of forty cubits in the
text of Day I. This fact probably indicates that the introduction of Noah's flood into this context is secondary. 28

The sentence tying Mount Tabor to Mount Olympus
seems to be incomplete. This prevents the precise ascer-
taining of the way in which the legend about Mount Olympus was related to the line of thought of this paragraph.
The height of Mount Tabor was apparently the point d'ap-
pui for the introduction of a short passage dealing with

---

28. The origins of the flood of fire are discussed in
the commentary to Day VII, supra. The continuation of
the text in the manuscript deals with the resolution of
a possible conflict between the covenant with Noah and
the future flood of fire. Inter alia it predicts that
for forty years before the day of judgement there will
be no rainbows because of the aridity which will prevail
at that time.

some traditions associated with Mount Olympus, traditions
designed to illustrate its great height. Its lofty ele-
vation was a subject of traditional lore as is clear from
Isidore of Seville's writings and other sources quoted
above. In them the idea is found that the mountain is so
high that the winds do not reach its peak. This forms
the first part of the tradition found in the Hebrew version of The Signs. The second part of the legend in The
Signs is without parallel known to this writer. Nonetheless, there seems no reason to doubt that it origina-
ted in some mediaeval embroidery on the legendary geogra-
phy of Greece. The absence of the birds and the need to
block the eyes and nostrils may have a relationship to
the thin atmosphere encountered at great heights.

Two textual comments may be made on this section. In
line 2, the reading   נתמלאה כל   is completely clear in the
manuscript. It is grammatically anomalous, however, and
perhaps is a case of wrong division for   נתמלא הכל   .
Second, the reading <האנ>יר   "the air" is somewhat con-
jectural; the first three letters alone are found in the
manuscript. Like אויר in line 12, the word here means
"the atmosphere" or perhaps even "the weather", showing
a semantic range like Greek ἀήρ, Latin aer.

Introduction (lines 11-16)

The second paragraph of the introduction is a sort
of summary of the text which follows. It introduces the
idea that the coming evils can be avoided by repentance,
an idea which finds no echo in any of the other texts and
seems to be out of place in view of the ideas of the document as outlined above.

In lines 14-15 the words translated "relate to his
son in fear that the day ..." could also be rendered
"relate to his son in fear. For the day ...".

In the text, the phrase   אשר לא יכילו זעמו   "which his
anger will not contain" is somewhat rough as it stands.

One might suppose that this goes back to a reading like
לא יכלה זעמו "his anger will not cease" (line 15).

Day I (lines 19-20): The actual text for the first day is
preceded by a second title which may be original to the
text, with the title to the introduction (line 1) having
been added together with the introduction.

The words "from the limit --- shores" should be compared with Jer 5:22. The expression rendered "rise to"
could be translated literally "increase to".

Day II (lines 20-21): This sign is identical in content
in the other versions. The word ישוכן "subsided" is that
used of the waters of the Flood in Gen 8:1. Corresponding to "until (they were) few", the other versions read
"to a depth" or "the depths" and also add an additional
clause.

Day III (lines 21-23): The mediaeval Hebrew form יתראו
corresponds to Latin apparentes. Hebrew reads merely"sea-
monsters", like the "whales" of B and I, not "fish and
whales", like C and II. The sea-monsters appear on the
face of the sea as in the Latin version, not on the face
of the "waters" like in the Armenian. The words מחוסר מים
    "because of the lack of water" are not paralleled in
the other versions. The word balaenas is added to explain what the תנינים were. This should be contrasted
with the belluae marinae of B and C.

Day IV (lines 23-25): This sign, the drying up of the
sea, is apparently equivalent to the burning of the sea
which is attested by all other versions. This shows the
structural similarity of the Hebrew version to the Latin
for in B and C texts this sign follows that of the
whales. In both Armenian texts the order is different
and this sign comes on Day VI.

Despite this, the text and content of this sign are

very different from those of the Latin and Armenian versions. It is probable that the text of Hebrew is secondary here, for the drying up of the sea is already implied by the sign of the second day in Latin and Armenian
and is stated actually to have taken place on that day by
the Hebrew version itself. This is why the whales are
stranded in the sign of Day III, and see in detail the
Commentary to these days above. The motive for the
transformation which the text has undergone in the Hebrew
version is not evident.

Day V (lines 25-27): The words "man and beast --- eyes"
have no obvious parallels. It should be noted that once
again Hebrew agrees with the Latin B and C which read
herbae et arbores, rather than with Armenian "trees".
This, together with the cases pointed out in the commentary here on other days, is a clear indication of the
relationship of the Vorlage of Hebrew with the type of
text preserved in Latin.

Day VI (line 25): This sign has no parallel in content in
Armenian and Latin B and C. In them, following the trees'
dripping blood is the portent of the destruction of buildings. In the Hebrew version this portent has been combined with the levelling of the mountains which occurs as
sign IX here and in the corresponding position in the
other versions. This perhaps is a result of the attempt
to organize the material more systematically, placing the
destruction of the buildings and the levelling of the
mountains after the great earthquake. It may also have
been facilitated by Ezek 38:20, see Day IX, below. The
word קולות could also be rendered "thunder", but this
translation has been used for the unambiguous רעמים
later in the sentence.

Day VII (line 28): The other versions do not have the
words "and melt". They might be compared to the "and be

destroyed" of Armenian II, but these seem more likely to be parallel, conjunctive developments rather than to reflect a common original.

Day VIII (lines 28-29): The text for this day is typical of the biblicizing character of the Hebrew version. Latin and Armenian have a prediction of an earthquake at this point. In Hebrew the verse 2 Sam 22:8 is quoted verbatim, with a reversal of the first two verbs. This caused the introduction of the shaking of the foundations of the heaven, a feature is drawn from that verse. The archaizing ending ון- of the final verb should be noted. It does not occur in the Massoretic text, but it is also found on the verb יבראון in the conclusion of The Signs and so is probably typical of the translator.

Day IX (lines 29-31): The composite nature of this material was noted in the observations on Day VI, supra. It might be suggested, in addition to the possibilities raised there, that the two Days were drawn together by the identity of the verb with which they both open, יפלו . In any case, the combination of the two texts is clear here. The other versions have the levelling of the mountains as the chief characteristic of this verse. Again, its love of biblical quotation comes to the fore when the Hebrew version draws its phrase for this from Ezek 38:20. This obscures somewhat the point of the portent which Latin formulates as aequabitur terra (C). On the origins of this expectation, see Commentary to Armenian, Day IX, above.

In 4 Ezra 5:5 the stones are said to give voice, but no clear parallels to this eschatological cry of the trees have been observed.[29]

29. The talking tree of T. Abr A3, B3 is of a quite different character, as are the parallels adduced by M. R. James, The Testament of Abraham ("Texts and Studies", II.2 ; Cambridge 1892) p. 59-64.

<u>Day</u> X (lines 31-32): The form of text for this day
found in Hebrew is almost a word for word quotation of
Isa 2:21 into which are incorporated two words from
Isa 2:19. The eschatological application of these verses became widespread, see the observations in the Commentary to Armenian, Day X, above. The text as presented in the Hebrew version, then, shows none of these
peculiar characteristics which distinguish the use of
this material in the Latin and Armenian traditions from
its uses in early Christian sources. In the Latin and
Armenian versions the portent is not men's concealment
in the crannies or the rocks, but their issuing forth
from them. Moreover, according to these two versions
those men who come forth from the rocks will be mad and
will run about and be unable to talk to one another.
Hebrew then provides a form of text which is both "biblicizing" and also in line with the more generally ac-
cepted understanding of the eschatological interpretation of these verses.[30]

<u>Day</u> XI (lines 32-33): The order of omens and days
agrees with Latin C and Armenian, not with Latin B. The
raising of the bones from the graves is couched in language drawn from Jer 22:19. The phraseology of Hebrew,
which refers to the bones, is like that of Latin, while
the Armenian version refers simply to "the dead".

<u>Day</u> XII (lines 33-35): In the other versions this sign
relates the falling of the stars and (according to
Latin B) of portents from the heavens. This has brought
Isa 34:4 to mind and the first part of this verse is
then quoted. The last part of the biblical verse,
however, refers to the "withering" of the heavenly host,

---

30. This interpretation does not seem to have been
current in Rabbinic sources, but it is nonetheless
ancient, see Commentary to Armenian Day X, <u>supra</u>.

using the word יבול . This word had two effects. The
first is that its phonetic similarity to יפולו "will
fall" used of the stars by The Signs provided an additional basis for association of Isa 34:4. At the same
time, this verbal root was the connection for the introduction of Isa 51:6. This combination of verses widens
the scope of the upheaval referred to in the other versions.

More difficult is the addition at the end of this
day. This talks first of an opening of the graves and
blowing of trumpets, and then quotes a little fragment
of Dan 12:3 apparently referring to a partial resurrection. Problematic is that all of this is followed by
the death of all men, then by the end of the world, new
creation, and resurrection of the dead; a more extensive
quotation from Dan 12:3 is used to the same end. The
various elements involved here are found in one or another place in the other versions, but not in the prophecy for this day or for this stage of the eschatological process. No explanation for the latter part of this
verse is evident, nor does it appear to conform to any
known eschatological pattern. On the role of the trumpet, see Commentary to Armenian, Day XV, above.

Day XIII (line 36): The death of all men is the common
content of this sign in the versions. Notable is a certain roughness in the Hebrew. The first verb is plural
and the second singular; a plural subject is not readily
evident. It is possible that יחד "together" is related
to a text of the type of Latin ut cum mortibus resurgent.
The actual phrase comes from Job 34:15.

Day XIV (line 36-fol. 257v line 1): The words "and melt
--- destroyed" have no parallels in the other versions.

Day XV (lines 1-6): In fact the first part of this text
is parallel to the other versions and to the beginning

of the quotation of Dan 12:2. This has been connected
to the words et resurgent omnes and then the following
verses strung onto it in such a way as to offer no convenient break at which one might nicely distinguish the
end of Day XV and the beginning of the concluding materials. In the translation, the start of the quotations
has been marked by an asterisk and their conclusion by
the verse reference in parentheses. The reference to
the valley of Jehosaphat as the place of judgement is
based on Joel 4:12 which is not quoted literally. The
last sentence is not biblical, except for the phrase
"the king, the Lord" (Ps 98:6). This section with its
catena of biblical citations bears a general resemblance
to the concluding comments in the text of Peter Comestor
with its New Testament excerpts.

PART TWO

ONOMASTICA SACRA

Introductory Remarks

In the Armenian tradition there was an extensive development of the Onomastica Sacra, the lists of biblical names together with their translations or "etymologies". Three Armenian lists of this were published by F. Wutz in 1914 - 1915[1]. The most extensive of these was his first list (hereinafter: Ona I). He edited this list, which contains 880 lines in the form published, on the basis of eight manuscripts. He published a second list, containing about 50 names and their explanations, on the basis of a single manuscript (Ona II), and a third, also drawn from a single manuscript contained 702 lines (Ona III). Up to the present, Wutz' is the only scholarly publication of these lists and in his book he attempts to locate them within the broader spectrum of the onomastic lists in various languages.

A second scholarly reference to these texts is by H.M. Amalyan in a book devoted to the extensive vocabularies, dictionaries, and onomastic lists found in mediaeval Armenian manuscripts. Evidently, Amalyan was not conscious of the existence of Wutz' study. In his book he lists a great many manuscripts of the Onomastica Sacra contained in the collection of the Matenadaran in Erevan, Armenia.

Wutz' study is marred by two faults. First, his published texts are based on a very limited range of manuscripts, as is evident from the list of manuscripts presented below. Second, his work is marked by very many typographical errors, chiefly in the Armenian text,

---

1. For bibliographical references, here and in the following, see the bibliographical list, pp. xiii-xvi above.

but occasionally in the notes. Moreover, the examination
of a broader range of manuscripts than he consulted
showed that there are other lists of which he was ignor-
ant. With all these reservations, however, his study
remains basic. Until there is a new, major edition of
those texts which he published, his edition is indispen-
sable. His analysis of all the onomastica in the various languages has no substitute.

A brief perusal of the appended, preliminary list
of manuscripts (Section VII, below) indicates that the
preparation of a complete and exhaustive edition of the
Armenian Onomastica Sacra would be a formidable task,
extending beyond the modest aims of the present work.
These are just to publish some new material, not included in the works of Wutz and Amalyan. These data are
drawn, primarily, from manuscripts in the library of the
Armenian Patriarchate of Jerusalem. To these manuscripts
have been added the texts contained in four codices in
the library of the Mechitarist Fathers in Venice, in one
codex from Paris not consulted by Wutz, and in one codex
from Erevan.[2] If these twenty one new manuscripts are
combined with the nine manuscripts used by Wutz, a total
of thirty manuscripts is reached.

Wutz, as observed above, published three different
lists, which have been dubbed here Ona I, Ona II, and
Ona III. New information is offered on his Ona I and
Ona III and on three unknown lists. These new lists are
the following:

Ona IV - A short list, contained in Paris, Bibliothèque
Nationale arm. 140 (no. 66). This list is a witness to
the long list (Ona I). It contains some elements additional to the long list, but these are not onomastic in

---

2. It is greatly to be regretted that only one of the
numerous copies in Erevan was available to the writer.
Any attempt to carry out a definitive study of the
lists would reauire consultation of a broader range
of the manuscripts of this rich treasury.

character. They are Armenian words, drawn from the Armenian Bible. The onomastic list upon which it was based
was particularly close to MS No. 1 of Ona I. A sample
of this list is given below, and its witness is also included in the apparatus of Ona I. (The numbers in par-
theses are those of Wutz' edition of Ona I.)

Ona V - Manuscripts nos. 55 and 81 (Venice, Mechitarist
545 and Erevan Matenadaran 2261) contain a new, previously unpublished list. This is edited in full below and a
commentary on it has been prepared, according to the following principles. The text of the list is based, chiefly, upon no. 81, and the text of no. 81 has been corrected or supplemented according to the text of no. 55 in
cases of clear corruption or omission. All variants of
nos. 55 or 81 have been recorded in full in the critical
apparatus. In cases of clear corruption of both manuscripts, the editor has corrected where he could, enclos-
ing his corrections in pointed brackets. This is again
noted in the apparatus.

     The commentary has been designed to show where a
name and etymology occur in Wutz' book and independent
observations have been added only where the name did not
occur in any of Wutz' sources. It is evident that this
list is akin to Ona III and the majority of the names
and etymologies given by it occur in that list. Ona V
does contain some additional elements not found in Ona
III and these include readings in common with Ona I,
readings in common with lists in other languages quoted
by Wutz (mainly Greek or Latin) and - of very consider-
able interest - readings not known in any of the onomastic sources quoted by Wutz. In the commentary attention has
been devoted, in particular, to these latter cases.

Ona VI - Jerusalem, Armenian Patriarchate 1422 (no. 82)
contains a major compilation of biblical onomastica and
vocabulary. This compilation covers almost 300 pages of

the manuscript. Following the entries for the first letter of the alphabet (ayb), the list for the same letter from another list has been added in the codex, with a scribal note indicating that this was something of an after-thought. This second list is drawn from an onomasticon. No similar separate supplement occurs for any other letter. In addition, the first list for ayb and ben contains a number of names, interspersed in rapidly increasing proportions with Armenian words and their dictionary meanings.

The list appended to ayb is, in fact, another copy of Wutz' Ona III, to which certain expansions have been added on the base of Ona I, and sample of it has been given below. The onomastic elements inserted into the biblical vocabulary in no. 82 proper are of a different character and two samples have been given, with translation and comments, under the title Ona VI. A few onomastic elements are to be found in the biblical vocabulary contained in Jerusalem, Armenian Patriarchate 1138 (1668 C.E.), pp. 283 f., but the list is primarily of Armenian words.

The Texts

The materials here published are then, in summary and in order of presentation:

Ona I - Four sample texts have been prepared based on Wutz' manuscripts and the following codices in our list: nos. 53, 54, 56, 57, 58, 59, 60, 61, 62, 63, 64, 65, 66, 78, 80, 83, 84. Observe that no. 64 contains the full text of Ona I expanded by elements of Armenian biblical vocabulary and of Ona VI (see below). These samples are:

i   The Preface, which precedes the list in all the manuscripts of it which were examined except   nos. 1, 7, 8, 57, 61, 64, 65.

ii   A list of the letters of the Hebrew alphabet and
      their explanation, which follows the Onomasticon
      in manuscript no. 1, follows the preface in most
      other copies examined, and is omitted by manuscripts
      nos. 7, 8, 55, 57, 64; no. 61 omits the names and
      gives only the explanations. The photograph of no.
      65 only includes the letters after k'ap'. To these
      witnesses, the text of no. 14, printed by Amalyan
      (p. 146) has been joined.

iii   The title of the list.

iv   A sample of the first forty names in Wutz' list. The
      text is that of Wutz. The above listed manuscripts
      were compared with this text, and their variants
      included in the critical apparatus. Moreover, Wutz'
      collations of nos. 5 and 7 were checked against the
      photographs as a control sample and his collations
      were found to be accurate, although marred by prin-
      ter's errors of which the chief are:

ln 7 apparatus *Ինշմանg*   for *Ինշմանg*,
ln 30 apparatus *շարշարվմ*   for *շարշարիմ*,
ln 32 apparatus *Արկրարվն*   for *Արկրաբիմ*,
ln 33 apparatus *պատասբանի* for *պատասխանի*.

Such errors have been corrected without further com-
ment and all other variants in Wutz' critical apparatus have been reproduced here. Manuscript no. 66
(Ona IV) does not include lns. 5, 6, 8, 9, 10, 12,
13, 14, 18, 20, 21, 22, 23, 24, 26, 27, 30, 31, 32,
34, 35, 37, 38, 39. The photographs of no. 64, were
unfortunately, incomplete and the following lns
were missing: 5, 9, 13, 14, 22, 23, 26, 27, 34, 35,
38, 40. A similar situation in manuscript 62 led
to the omission of lns 13, 15, 23, 24. None of
these omissions are noted in the apparatus.

v.   In addition to the sample texts, tables have been prepared which enable a comparison of the order of names in the manuscripts. As will be evident from the tables, there are a number of different ways in which the names were arranged in the list of this type and these may provide one of the keys for grouping its textual families. These tables contain the first fifty names in the list, and, after the first column in which the names are transliterated and assigned numbers, the numbers alone are given.   Only major variants in the form of the names are noted.   An unnumbered blank space indicates an omission.

Ona III - A sample of text, forty names in scope, is given with appropriate comparisons with Wutz' text and Ona V in the commentary and all variants of Wutz' text in the apparatus.

Ona IV - As a sample of text, the full collations of letters ayb and ben are given. The numbers in parentheses are those of the occurrence of the item in Ona I, from which, as noted above, Ona IV has been excerpted. No commentary is appropriate in view of the secondary character of the list.   The unnumbered items are all elements of Armenian biblical vocabulary and are added following the onomastic material.

Ona V - This new list is published in full with translation and commentary.   Its sources and character have already been described.

Ona VI - The existence Ona VI no. 82 was mentioned above.   With the readings of this manuscript are allied certain of the readings of no. 64, particularly where nos. 82 and 64 are opposed to Ona I.   All readings common to the two manuscripts have been compared and for Sample i the variants of no. 64 included an apparatus.   It thus appears that no. 64 is a witness both to Ona I and to Ona VI.

Sample i is composed of the first forty items in no. 82. The ratio of names is certainly higher than in the rest of the text, but Armenian words, Greek words, and one Hebrew word are also included. The totals are:

Onomastic elements	– 23
Armenian words	– 11
Greek words	– 4
Hebrew words	– 1
Inexplicable	– 1

The characteristics of the onomastic elements are examined in the commentary. A further group of names from the letter ben was also examined (Sample ii). The distribution of co-incidence of the onomastic elements found in these two samples drawn from Ona VI with the various Armenian lists is tabulated here. It should be borne in mind that sometimes one single entry of Ona VI combines different etymologies.

Agreement with:	No. of cases:	
Ona I	11	(i 1,4,6,11,14,21,25,27; ii 9,6,7,8)
Ona II	2	(i 14,21)
Ona III	6	(i 3,5,27,29,30; ii 5)
Ona V	4	(i 27; ii 3,7)
No parallels but explicable	6	(i 10,24,28,31,32; ii 4)
inexplicable	10	(i 2,17,21,22,38,39,40; ii 1)
expansionary	3	(i 4,25,27).

It follows that Ona VI is a list drawn from varied sources - onomastica, Greek-Armenian lexica, Armenian-Armenian lexica, and perhaps a list of Hebrew transliterations. Moreover, an analysis of its onomastic elements shows a great diversity. Not only are the chief onomastica known to us reflected, but Ona VI also contains some biblical onomastic elements not known in Wutz' sources and even some further, unidentifiable onomastic elements of unknown character.

It should further be noted that the <u>Dictionary</u>
edited by Eremia <u>vardapet</u> (1728) has incorporated a list
of words resembling Ona VI, apparently drawn from a manuscript source.

It lists all the items included in the samples offered
here, except for   i   28 (but see commentary), 31,39 and
40. It cannot be used, therefore, as an independent lex-
icographic source, but may serve as a witness to the
manuscript tradition (compare note on Ona VI ln 37,
below). It should be noted, moreover, that this dictionary also contains onomastic elements in addition to Ona
VI, including material like Ona I and Ona III. It is
worthy of closer examination by future editors of <u>Onomas-</u>
<u>tica</u> <u>Sacra</u> <u>Armenica</u>.

<u>List of Manuscripts</u>: This list does not claim to be
exhaustive, but it is a rather inclusive listing of manuscripts containing onomastic lists and establishes a
series of numbers by which they are referred to throughout this study. It is suggested that this list form the
basis for future editions and studies.

<u>Index of Names</u> follows at the conclusion of this
section.

Transcription of the Names

All names are transcribed exactly according to the
system set forth above. It should be observed that in
Armenian <u>ov</u> often corresponds to Greek ω. Scribal prac-
tice is, moreover, often to add a <u>y</u> to final <u>a</u> and <u>o</u>.
This is a graphic convention, not reflected in tradition-
al pronunciation. Moreover, confusion of the sounds in
each of the following series is not uncommon, <u>d</u>, <u>t</u>, <u>t</u>:
<u>g</u>, <u>k</u>, <u>k</u>; <u>b</u>, <u>p</u>, <u>p</u>. All of these phenomena remain in the
text and translation exactly as in the manuscripts
except that final, otiose <u>y</u> is omitted.

ONA I

SAMPLES OF TEXT

i Preface

Այս բառք բաղաձայնք. Հոմանուանց բազմածեալ, զամենայն
որ ինչ միանգամ (են) անուանք Հեբրայեցի յաւրէն եւ ի
մարգարէս. եւ ի նոր կտակարանս թարգմանեալ եւ մեկնեալ
յեբրայեցւոյն ի յոյնս եւ ի յունէն ի Հայս կարգաւ ըստ
5   նշանագրաց ալփաբէթիցն եբրայեցւոց թէ զինչ միաբա-
նութիւն անուանց ունիցին:

1   բարբա 54   բառ 78   + եռաՀիւսական 2 5 6 84
     + յեռաՀիւսական 53 56 59 62 78 79 83 | բաղաձայն
     84   բակծածեալ 78 83   բակծածեալք 79   բակծայնեալք
     84 | ամենայն   78 79
2   որ ինչ միանգամ}   om 53* 78   ինչ որ են 56 59 62
     ինչ որ 78 83 | յեբրայեցի 83 84 | յաւրէնս 53
     54 56 58 59 60 62 63 79 80 84
4   յեբրայեցւոցն 54 56 59 60 62 63 83   յեբրայեցոց
     84   յեբրայեցւոյ 79 | յոյնս} յոյն 78 | յունէն
     յունաց 59 62   յունացն 60   յունացս 80 | Հայս}
     Հայ 78 79 80 83 84   + յասորի եւ ասորւոց 2

This consonant lexicon translated and interpreted all
the names which (are) in the Hebrew Law and Prophets and
in the New Testament, including homonyms, from Hebrew
into Greek and from Greek into Armenian, in order by the
letters of the alphabet of the Hebrews, whatever agreement of names (i.e. meaning) they might have.

5 *Նշանագրաց} Նշանագրացն* 79 84 *եւ զմեկնութիւն*
   Նշանագրաց (Նշանագրացն 83 84) 2 5 6 53^c 83 |
   լփափեից 2 *ալֆա* 54 60 63 *ալֆաբեթիցն* 79 80 84
   այբբեմից 83 | *երրայեցոց* 84 | *միաբանութիւն}*
   մեկնութիւն 81
6 *ունիցին անուանց* 59 62 | *անուանց}* om 79
   անուանցն 83 | *ունին* 78

ii Alphabet

1	Ալեփ.	ուսումն նշանագրաց:
	Բեթ.	բնակեա ի դմայ:
	Քամիլ.	լրումն վերագոյն {կամ ծնունդ}:
	Դալեթ.	գրեալք բարձագոյնք:
5	Հէ.	սայ:
	Վաւ.	ի սմանէ:
	Զէ.	եկեաց:
	Խեթ.	կենդանի է:
	Տեթ.	բարի է:
10	Յովդ.	սկիսբն:
	Քաբ.	դենելս:
	Դամեդ.	ուսիր:
	Մեմ.	ի սմանէ:
	Նուն.	յալիտենից:
15	Սամբաթ.	աւգնականութիւն:
	Եգ.	աղբեալրական:
	Փէ.	բերան:
	Ծադէ.	զարդարութիւն:
	Կոփ.	կոչումն սրբութեան:
20	Րեշ.	երեւելի կամ առաջնորդ:
	Շին.	ատամունք:
	Թաւ.	նշան կամ կոչումն:

1	Alep',	teaching of letters.
	Bet',	dwell in it!
	K'amil,	upper fullness or birth .
	Daɫet',	higher writings.
5	Hē,	this.
	Vaw,	from this.
	Zē,	he lived.
	Xet',	he is living.
	Tet',	he is good.
10	C'ovd, (corr. for Yovd)	beginning.
	K'ab,	still.
	Ɫamed,	learn!
	Mem,	from this.
	Nun,	eternal.
15	Samk'aɫ',	helpfulness.
	Ec', (corr. for Ey)	of a spring.
	P'ē,	mouth.
	Cadɛ,	ornamentation.
	Kap',	call of sanctity.
20	Reš,	visible or first.
	Šin,	teeth.
	T'aw,	sign or call.

1 om 60 | Ալիփ 2 4 5 6 14 56 59° Ալլիփ 3 Աղիփ 53
78 Ալիֆ 54 58 59ˣ 62 63 79 80 84 Աղէֆ 83 |
ուսումն } + բանագրաց կամ 53 56 59 62 | նշանագրացն
79

2 Բէթ 3 4 14 53 54 56 58 59 60 62 78 80 83 84
Բէղ 2 | բնակեալ 56 83 բնա 59 62 | դմին 14
դմաց 54 դմա 79 80 83

3 Գամիղ 3 4 14 53 56 58° 59 62 63 80 84 Գամիլ 54 60
79 Գամեղ 78 83 Կամիղ 58* | լրումն վերագոյն }
om 2 | լրումն} + լրումն 61 | վերագուն 54 58

4 Դաղէթ 3 4 14 53 56 60 63 80 83 Դալէթ 59 Դալեթ 62
Դալեղ 2 (?) Գաղէթ 54 58 Անէթ 79 Դալէթ 84 + ծնունդ
կամ 83 | գրեալ 59 62 | բարձագոյնք} բարձր 2-5
14 53 54 56 58 59 60 62 63 78 79 80 83 84 + կամ
ծնունդ 3 4 5 14 53* 54 56 58 59 60 62 63 78 79 80
om 6 + կամ շալիղ շնորիաց 53ᶜ

5 սա 79 80

6 ի սմանէ } ըմանէ 6

7 գային 9 գի 79 | կեաց 3-6 14 53 54 56 58 59
60 62 63 78 79 80 84 կայց 2 կեայց 61 83

8 եթ 2 79 Հեթ 6 Խէթ 14 53 54 56 58 59 60 62 63 |
է } om 78

9 Տէթ 2-6 14 53 54 56 58 59 60 62 63 78 83 | om tot
79 84

10 Յոդ 3 4 54 56 58 60 63 80 Յող 6 Յոտ 2 5 14 53 59
62 78 83 իոդ 84 | սկիզբն 2-6 53 54 56 58-63 78-80
83 84

11 Քափ 4 5 53 54 56 58 59 62 63 65 78 80 83 Քասփ 3
ⵑ յասի 2 | դերեւ 3

12 Լամեբ 2 5 56 59 60 62 Լամէբ 4 58 84 Լամեզ 3 63 80
Լամէզ 65 Լամէթ 6 Մաղէբ 53ᶜ Լամեթ 78

13 Մէմ 6 56 83 | Մեմ tantum post ln 22 84 |
ի մասնէ 59

14 ուն 2 նու 59 62 նոյն 83 | յալիտեան 2-6 14 53 54
56 58-63 65 78 79 80 83 84

15 Սամէբ 6 Մամբամ 59 62 | օգնականութիւն 54 60 61 78

```
      79 84   օգնութիւն 59   աւգնութիւն 53* 58* 65   -ական-
      53° 58°  յօգնութիւն 62
16    էg 2 53* 59 62 65   էյ 3 4 5 53c 54 56 58 60 63 80
      83  յ 79  էյ 84  Ային 6  |  աղերակն 2 4 5 14 54
      58 59 62 63 65 78-80 83 84   աղիւր ակն 61 աղերական
      3  ողբերաւոր 6  |  + կամ եղբայր ՟այական 56  |+ կամ
      եղբայր կայական 59 62 65
18    ազէ 2  ծազէ 53* 54 65 78 83  Սաղէ 6  |  զօրութիւն
      59
19    Կոփ 6  Քուփ 84  |  սրբութիւն 54* 79  |  + կամ
      կոշումն ՟եթանսաց սրբոց 53 56 59 62 65  |  + կամ
      երեւելի 61
20    Րէ2 2-6 53 54 56 58 60 78   էշ 79 80 83 84  |
      երեւելի կամ} om 61  |  որ երեւել 62  |  կամ} om 2-
      6 14 53 54 56 58 59 60 62 63 65 78-80 83 84
21    ին 2  |  աղամունք 3
22    Թափ 1  |  նշանակ 61  |  նշան կամ} om 2  |  կոշումն}
      կանշումն 4 5 53c 54 58 60 63* 79 84  կամ կանշումն 3
```

Note that Wutz' text apparently contains two misprints
in the apparatus to no. 22: կանմուէ^n for կանշուՄն and
կամ կամշուՄն for կամ կանշուՄն . No. 79 has not entered
the initial letters, from ln. 8 to the end of the alphabet. These **readings** are not recorded above.

In Erevan 1500, the famous Miscellany written by Mexitar of Ayrivank, on p. 370, as an enumeration of the books of the Bible, the letters of the Hebrew alphabet are found. Since they are close, in their form, to the tradition of the onomastica, they are also given here.

Ալիփ: Բեթ: Գամեղ: Դաղեթ: Հէ: Վաւ: Զէ: Խէթ: Տեթ:

Յաւտ: Քափ: Ղամէթ: Մեմ: Նուն: Սամքաթ: Է: Փէ:

Ծագէ: Կոփ: Րեշ: Շին: Թաւ:

Alip', Bet', Gameł, Dałet', Hē, Vaw, Zē, Xet',Tet',

Yawt, K'ap', Łamēt', Mem, Nun, Samk'at', Ē, P'ē,

Cagē, Koḍ, Reš, Šin, T'aw.

iii Title

(1)   *Բանք եբրայեցւոց*

բանք } + բսա 2 60   + գիրք   7 | այս բանք 6 | եբրայեց-

ngն 78   եբրայեցւոցն 80

(2)   *Զայս բանս եբրայեցի Յանունանց ՚Յետեւողին առաբելոց*

          Փիլոնեայ Թարգմանեալ էին ի լեզու յոյն:

Thus only 1. Title is omitted completely by no. 84.

(1) Words of the Hebrews

(2) These words of Hebrew names were translated into

Greek by Philo who succeeded the Apostles.

1   Ադամ.   երկիր կոյս կամ երկիր մարմնացեալ
{կամ յերկրէ կամ երկիր կարմիր}:

2   Աբել.   գլորշի սգոյ {յաստուծոյ տուեալ
մարգարէութիւն}:

3   Ադդա.   վայելի կամ վկայութիւն նոցա:

4   Արփաքսադ.   մարգարէութիւն տեսանել {մաքրութիւն
տեսանելի}:

5   Ասուր.   բերէզգոհոմն կամ միջագետք:

6   Աբրամ.   հայր մեծարոյ կամ հայր բարձրեալ կամ
վերամբարձ:

7   Աբրահամ.   հայր ազգաց կամ հայր ընտրեալ:

8   Ազար.   սայ պանդուխտ:

9   Աւնան.   վնասեալ սրտիւ:

10   Ամարփադ.   խստութիւն չար կամ չարութիւն:

11   Աբիմեղեք.   հաւր իմոյ արքայութիւն:

12   Ամմովն.   ժողովուրդ նոցա կամ որդի ազգի:

13   Ասեր.   վարձք կամ մեծութիւն կամ երանութիւն:

14   Արամ.   անէծք նոցա:

15   Ասաթ.   հաւատ:

16   Ամինադաբ.   ազգ ցանկալի:

17   Ազազ.   որթ:

18   Ամրամ.   հայր բարձրելոյ կամ ժողովուրդ
մեծի:

19   Ահարովն: ահա հոգի:

1   Adam,   virgin earth or incarnated earth

{or from earth or red earth}.

2   Abel,   vapour of mourning {prophecy given

by God}.

3   Adda,   ⌐enjoyable⌐ (<u>corr. for</u> witnessing)

or their witness.

4   Arp'ak'sad, to see prophecy {visible cleanliness}

5   Asur,   ⌐<u>unknown word</u>⌐ or Mesopotamia.

6   Abraam,   honoured father or elevated father

or exalted.

7   Abraham,   father of nations or elect father.

8   Agar,   this sojourner.

9   Awnan,   harmed by (at) heart.

10   Amarp'ał   bad straitness or evil.

11   Abimełek',   my father's kingdom.

12   Ammovn,   their people or son of nation.

13   Aser,   reward or greatness or beatitude.

14   Aram,   their curses.

15   Asat',   faith

16   Aminadab,   desirable nation

17   Agag,   vine.

18   Amram,   father of most high or people of

great one.

19   Aharovn,   behold a spirit.

20   Աբիդան.   ծառայութիւն:

21   Աբիրամ.   եղբայր իմոյ բարձրութիւն:

22   Ասրովն.   տապանակ:

23   Առած.   պատզամ:

24   Ափփուսովթ. ծածուկ:

25   Անթրակ.   . . .

26   Արիովն.   իշխան կամ կատարեալ:

27   Ասերովն.   երանութիւն կամ ʿՉուիթʾ կատարեալ:

28   ԱմուրՂացի. ծաղեալք:

29   Ամաղեք.   ազգ լեզունող:

30   Աղոնիբեզեկ. տէր շարշարից:

31   Ազան.   յայնժամ այսբ:

32   Ակրաբիմ.   կարճիք:

33   Անաթովթ.   պատասխանի:

34   Արուէր.   ընդղեմ աստուծոյ:

35   Աւովղ.   խոստովանելի:

36   Աննա.   արարած նոցա:

37   Ազոտոս.   Ղրածին կամ . . .

38   Ասկալովն.   կշրեալ:

39   Ակկարոն.   ամլութիւն:

40   Արիմաթեմ.   լերինք:

20	Abidan,	servitude.
21	Ak'iram,	elevation of my brother.
22	Asrovn,	ark.
23	Aŕac,	command.
24	Ap'p'usovt',	secret.
25	Ant'rak,	...
26	Ariovn,	prince or perfect.
27	Aserovn,	beatitude or perfect ⌈David⌉ (<u>corr.</u> <u>for</u> 'forecourt').
28	Amurhac'i,	having mocked.
29	Amałek',	licking nation.
30	Adonibezek,	lord of sufferings.
31	Asan,	then these.
32	Akrabim,	scorpions.
33	Anato'vt',	answer.
34	Aruēr,	against God.
35	Awovd,	confessing.
36	Anna,	their creation.
37	Azotos,	born of fire or . . .
38	Askalovn,	weighed.
39	Akkaron,	barrenness.
40	Arimat'em.	mountains.

1   երկիր կոյս} երկիր կամ երկիր կոյս 2 6 53^{C} 61 64 78
երկիր (om 56) կամ կոյս 3 4 5 8 53* 54 56 58 62 63
65 66 83 84 | կամ երկիր- fin } om 66 | մարմնա-
ցեալ 65 մնացեալ 79 | երկիր կամ մարմնացեալ 56 |
երկիր կարմիր կամ յերկրէ (երկրէ 78) 7 53 54 56 57
59 60 62 63 65 78 79 80 83 84 | + առաւել 7

2   Աբէլ 83 84 | գոլորշի սգոյ} om 2 5 6 57 61 66 78-
80 84 | յաստուծոյ- fin} om 83 | յաստուծոյ }
աստուծոյ 54 78 յայտնեալ 53* 65 + եւ յայտնեալ 56
+ յաստուծոյ տուեալ 53^{C} | մարգարէութիւն } + կամ
տեսանելի 3-6 8 53 54 56 58 59 60 62-65 79 80 |
+ կամ տեսութիւն կամ տեսանելի 84 | + կամ գոլոշի
(գոլոշէ 65 գորշի 56* գոլորշի 56° 63 64) սգոյ
կամ գուլթ վերաբերեալ (վերաբերել 56 65) կամ երկիր
(om 64) բազմաբեր 3 4 8 53 54 56 58-60 62-65 79
80 84

3   Ադէն 2 6 57 Ադէ 78 Ադին 5 79 Ագռա 83 | վայելել
2 5 6 վկայելի 4 8 53 57 59 61 62 64 83 84 վկելի
3 վայելէ 59 79 | կամ} ի 2 5 6 57 78 79 |
վկայութեան 2 5 6 | նոցա} om 2-8 53 57 59 61 62
64 80 83 84 | + Ադին (Ադային 59 62) վկայելել
(վայել է 54 58-63) ի վկայութիւն նոցա (աստուծոյ 57
om 53 marg) 3 4 7 53 marg54 56-66 | + փափկութիւն
5

4   om totum 84 Արփաքսաթ 59 61 80 Արփազսաթ 53 marg|
տեսանելի tantum 80 | մարգարէութիւն տեսանել} om
2 57 66 | մարգութիւն 3 | տեսանել} տեսանելի
3-8 53 54 56 58-63 65 78 83 | մաքրութիւն
տեսանելի } om 3-8 53 54 56 58-63 65 78 80 |

5   բարեգոնման 53* 59 60 62 63 բարեգոնման 3 4 8 54
բերեգոնումն 5 7 56 57 61 62 78 80 84 բերոյ գոնումն
53 marg բարեգոնումն 79 բերեգամ 83 | բերեգոնման-
fin} om 58 | միշագետք } + կամ խորհուրդք 3 4 7 8
53 54 56 60 63 65 79 80 + կամ (om 58) խորհուրդք
(խորհուրդ 84) սուրբ 5 58 84 + խորհուրդք 59 |
միշագետ խորհուրդս 62

6   Աբրահամ 54   57 65   Աբրասամ 61 | մեծապրւ 78 |
     կամ 1°- fin } om 83 | կամ-բարձրեալ} om 2-8 53 54
     56-65 78 79 80 84 | կամ 2°} om 59 62 | վերամ-
     բարձ } վէմ ամբարձ 59 62 | + վասն աստեղ 7

7   Աբրասամ 2-4 6 7 56 58-60 63 80 84   Աբրայամ 8 |
     ազգեաց 2 7 8 65 | հայր 2°} om 8 | կամ հայր
     ընտրեալ }   om 6 57 61 64 66   կամ ընտրեալ հնչմանց
     2-4 7 53 54 56 58 60 63 65 78-80 83 84   կամ
     հնչմանց կամ ընտանաւորեալ 62   կամ հնչմանց կամ
     ընտւլ. 59 | + վասն իմաստասիրական բանից եւ
     գործոց 7

8   Ագարսա: պանդուխտ 56 57 | սա 78-80 84 | պան-
     տուխտ 78   պանդուխ 83

9   վնասեւ 83 | սրտի 65

10   Ամարփին 7   Ամարադ 57 Ամրափադ 78 | խիստութիւն 6 |
     չար- fin}   om 84 | չար} om   2-8 53 54 56-65 78-80
     83 | + Ամարբախ խստութիւն կամ չարութիւն 8 59 62

11   Աբիմելեք 5 61   Աբիմելէք 6-8 56 58 59 62 63 66 78
     80 83   Աբիմեղէք 4 53 65   Աբիմելիք 2 54 57   Աբիմէլէլ
     3   Աբիմէլէք 60 79 84 | յարբայութիւն 64

12   Ամոմն 2   Ամովն 64   Ամմոն 3-5 7 53 56 59 60 62 63
     79 80 84   Ամոն 6 54 57 61 65   Ամնովն 78   Ամոն
     83 | ժողովուրդք 62   ժողովւրանց 64 | նոցա }
     աստուծոյ 3 om   54   illeg 58 | կամ-ազգի } om 78

13   Ասէր 2 83 | վարձ կամ} om 2-8 53 54 56-61 63 65
     66 78-80 83 84 | երանութիւն} երկայնութիւն 3 4
     8 53 marg 54 56 58-60 62 63 80 84 | + կամ գովիչ
     79

14   om 79 84

15   om omn

16   Ամինադաւ 2   Ամինադամ 64* | + նա 7

17   om omn elsewhere   Աղադ (Աղաց 53*   Ագադ 61) երինչ
     (էրինչ 65) 2-8 53 54 56-65 78-80 83 | + Ագագ
     (Ագադ 65) երինչ (երինչ 7) 3 7 8 53 56 59 62 64 65 |
     + կամ երկիւղ 3 53

18   Ամրամ 1*   Արամ 54   Ամրան 79 | բարձրացելոյ 7 53 57

59-63 78-80 84 բարձրելոց 53ᶜ | ժողովուրդք 62 |
մեծի} բարձր omn

19 Աշարոն 7 56 57 63 65 Աշարան 6 | աշա} + լեանն
կամ շողի կամ բան (բերան 2 64) 2 6 57 61 64 66 |
շողի} + կամ լեանն 83   + կամ լեանն կամ (+ կամ 5)
բան (բանն 60) 4 5 7 8 53 54 56 58-60 62 63 65 78-
80 84 | + ΙΑ] բարիմ եղբայր բարձր 8

20 Աբիթան 3-5 7 8 53* 54 56 58-60 62-65 79 80 84 |
Աբիզան 83

21 om 84 | Աքարիմ 3 4 7 58 59 62 63 79 80 |
եղբայր իմ (om 2 79) բարձր omn: cf ln 19

22 Արոն 3-6 8 53 56 58-63 65 78-80 83 84 Արովն 2 57
Արան 7 Արսն 54

23 + թիւ 5

24 om 2 5 6 7 53 54 56 61 65 66 78 83 | ի ծածուկ
3 4 8 58-60 63 79 80 84

25 om omn

26 Ասերովն 2-5 7 8 54 56 58-63 78-80 84 Ասերոն 6
Ասէրոն 56 Ասրովն 83 | իշխանք կամ (om 54 56)
կատարեալք (կատարեալ 59 62) 2-8 53 54 56-63 65
78-80 83 84

27 Ասերովբ 2 Ասերովթ 3-8 53 56-63 65 78-80 83 84
Ասերով 54 | դալիթ} գալիթ 2 4-7 53* 54 56-58 60
63 65 78 80 գալիթ 79 + կամ 53ᶜ

28 Ամուբշացիք 2 3 5 6 61 64 78 Ամուրշացի 54 |
ծաղեալ} չեղեալք (om 2 չեղեալ 57 61 62 66 78 80
չեղեալք 54 58 60 63 80* գեղեալ 64 ծախեալք 53ᶜ 56
58) կամ ծաղեալք (ծաղեալ 57 61 66 78 80) 2-8 53 54
56-64 66 78-80 83 84

29 Ամաղէկ 2-4 8 54 57-60 62 63 65 66 78-80 83 Ամաղեկ
6 | լեգուանoդ 79 լեգուաւդ 80 լիգոդ 83

30 Աղովնիբեզեկ 5 Աղoնիբեզեկ 7 Աղոնիգեբեկ 54 58 |
չարչարից } 1 60 չարչարիմ 2 արարիչ 56 չարչարի
78 չարչարիչ rel

31 յայնժամ աժժամ 64 + կամ 60 + ժ. 2 | այսք } ազգ
2 78

32 Արկրաքիմ 3   Աշրաքիմ 7   Ակրաթիմ 58   Ակրապիմ 65
    Ակրափիմ 84 | կարիՖ 3 4 8 58 59 62-64 79 80 84
    կարիւք 2

33 Անապովթ 53 66   Անայթովթ 62

34 Արուէլ 2 3 5 7 54 56 59 60 62 63 65 80 84   Արուէլ
    8 (sic Wutz)   Արուէր 4   Անւէլ 58   Արուէլ 78
    Արուէդ 79 | ընդդեմ} + յաննել 2-5 7 53c 54
    56 57 59 60 61 63 65 78 79 80 83   + աննել
    8 53 * 62 84 | յասաուծոյ 58
    յասաուծոյ 58

35 Աւոդ 2   Աւովթ 3 4 8 53 54 58 59 60 62 63 80 83 84
    Աւաւէթ 7   Արոդ 57 | խոսաովանեալ 54

36 Աննա } om 54| Աննայ 78 84 | արարածոց 53 |
    նոցա } 1 նորա (նորայ 80) omn

37 Ագոտովս 2-8 53 54 56 58-65   Ագովատս 78-80 83 84
    Ագովատվ 57 | Ֆրածին} Ֆայրածին 3 | կամ} om 53
    54 56-65 78-80 83 84

38 Ասկադոն 2-4 6-8 53 54 56-63 65 79 80 84   Ասկադով
    78   Ասկադովն 5 53   ԱսկադոՀն 83 | կշոեալ 2 4-7 53
    54 56-65 78-80 83 84   կշոեալ 3 (sic Wutz)

39 om 84 | Ակկարովն 5 78 83 | ամրութիւն 6

40 Արեմաթեմ 3 57 66   Արիեմաթեմ 62   Արեմմաթեմ 5
    Արիմաթէմ 65 79°   Արիմաթիմ 79   Արիմմաթեմ 83 |
    լերինք} + preceding բարձրութիւն կամ 2-8 53 54
    56 57 58 60 61 63 65 66 78 79 80 83 +preceding
    բարձրութիւնք կամ 8 53 59 62 լերանց 8 59 62

ONA I v A TYPE I : ORDER OF NAMES

No. 65 Nos. 63, 80 No. 54	No. 58	No. 60	No. 56	No. 7	No. 79	Name
1 Ադամ	1	1	1	1	1	Adam
2 Ադին	2	2	2	2	2	Adin
3 Ադին	3	3	3	3	3	Adin
4 Ադոնիբեզեկ	4	4	4	4	4	Adonibezek
					Ադոնիրամ	(Adoniram)
					Ադրամելէք	(Adramelēk)
5 Ադդեր	5	5	5	5	7	Adder
6 Ադրաազար	6	6	6	6	8	Adraazar
7 Ադրամելէք	7	7	7	7		Adramełek'
8 Ադովնայ	8	8	8	8	9	Adovna
9 Ադովնիայ	9	9	9	9	10 Ադնան	Adovnia (VL Adina)
10 Ադի	10	10	10	10	11	Adi
11 Ադոնիէլ	11	11	11	11	12	Adoniēl
12 Ադադ	12	12	12	12	13	Adad
				13 Ադամ		(Adam)
13 Ադդա	13	13	13	14	14	Adda
14 Աբէլ	14	14	14	15	15	Abēl
15 Աբրահամ	15	15	15	16	16	Abraham (VL Abram)
16 Աբարամ	16	16	16	17	17	Abaram (VL Abraham)
17 Աբիմէլէք	17	17	17	18	18	Abimełek'
18 Աբիթան	18	18	18	19	19	Abit'an

№	Armenian						№	Latin
19	Աբիգեայ	19	19	19	19	19	20	Abigea
20	Աբիաթար	20	20	20	20	20	21	Abiat'ar
21	Աբեսողոմ	21	21	21	21	21	22	Abĕsałom
22	Աբեննէր	22	22	22	22	22	23	Abennēr
23	Աբենեզեր	23	23	23	23	23	24	Abenēzer
24	Աբիդդար	24	24	24	24	24	25	Abiddar
25	Աբեղմայուռայ	25	25	25	25	25	26	Abełmayuła
26	Աբբիայ	26	26	26	26	26	27	Abbia
27	Աբդիու	27	27	27	27	27	28	Abdiu
28	Աբիոն	28	28	28	28	28	29	Abion
29	Աբբանա	29	29	29	29	29	30	Abbana
		30 Ապապովթ	30 Ապապովթ	30Ապապովթ	30Ապապովթ	31Ababovt'ə		(Ababovt')
30	Աբիսակ	31	31	31	31	30	31	Abisak
31	Աբբա	32	32	32	32	31	32 33Աբբայ	Abba (Abbray)
32	Աբրաթ	33	33	33	33	32	33 34Աբբայ	Abrat' (Abray)
33	Աբանմայ	34	34	34	34	33	34	Abana
34	Աբեղ 35Աբբաէղ	35Աբբատ	35Աբբել	35Աբբաէ	34Աբբ	35Աբրատ'ը	35 36Աբբաէղ	Abeł (VL Abbaēl)
35Աբբաէղ		36	35	34Աբբ	35	36		
36	Աբիուրիմ	37	36	35	36	37	36	Abiuzim
37	Աբեղբի	38	37	36	37	38	37	Abełbi
38	Աբիուդ	39	38	37	38	39	38	Abiud
39	Աբեղա	40	39	38	39	40	39	Abeła
40	Աբրոս		40	39	40		40	Abrot (Abot)
				40			41	

	41 Աբբոք	41 Աբբոք	41 Աբբոք	41 Աբբոք	40 Աբաբովթ 41 Աբբոք			
40 Ազար	42	42	42	42	42		42	(Ababovt')
41 Ազագ							43	(Abrok)
42 Ագռամթովն	43	43	43	43	43			Agar
					44 Ազազ		44	Agag
43 Ագաբոս	44	44	44	44	45			Agṙamt'ovn
44 Արփաքսաթ	45	45	45	45	46		45	(Agag)
45 Արաբովթ	46	46	46	46	47			Agabos
46 Արամ	47	47	47	47	48			Arp'ak'sat'
47 Արուէլ	48	48	48	48	49			Arabovt'
48 Արիմաթէմ	49	49	49	49	50			Aram
49 Արքեղաւոս	50	50	50	50				Aruēl
50 Արիսպագոս								Arimat'em
								Ark'eławos
								Arispagos

46 Ազովր (Azovr)
47 Ազան (Azan)
48 Ազովկոս (Azovtos)
49 Ազայէլ (Azayēl)
50 Ազայզայէլ (Azayzayēl)

ONA I v B TYPE II : ORDER OF NAMES

No. 5	No. 57	No. 61	No. 78	No. 83	
1 Ադամ	1	1	1	1	Adam
2 Աբէլ	2	2	2	2	Abēl
3 Ադին	3	3	3 Արէ	3	Adin (Adē)
4 Արփաքսադ	4	4	4	4	Arp'ak'sad
5 Ասուր	5	5	5	5	Asur
6 Աբրամ	6 Աբրաամ	6 Աբրահամ	6	6	Abram (VL Abraham)
7 Աբրահամ	7	7	7	7	Abraam
8 Ագար	8	8	8		Agar
9 Աւնան	9	9	9	8	Awnan
10 Ամարփաղ	10	10	10 Ամրաֆաղ	9	Amarp'ał (VL Amra-p'ał)
11 Աբիմելէք	11	11	11	10	Abimelek'
12 Ամմովն	12	12	12	11 Ամնոն	Ammovn (Amnon)
13 Ասեր	13		13	12	Aser
		13 Աբբենելէք			(Abimelik')
14 Արամ	14	14	14	13	Aram
				14 Ագար	Agar
15 Ամինադաբ	15	15	15	15	Aminadab
16 Ամրամ	16	16	16	16	Amram
17 Ահարովն	17	17	17	17	Aharovn
18 Աբիթան	18	18		18	Abit'an
19 Աբիդար	19 Աբիդար	19 Աբեդար			(Abidar)

			18 Ամարոն		(Aharon)
19 Ասերովթ	20	20	19		Aserovt'
			20 Ադին		(Adin)
20 Աքիրամ	21	21	21 Աքիրամ	19	Ak'iram (Abiram)
21 Ասերովն	22	22	22	20	Aserovn
				21 Ասրովն	(Asrovn)
22 Ամուրհացիք	23	23	23	22	Amurhac'ik'
23 Ամաղեկ	24	24	24	23	Amałek
24 Ադովնիբեզեկ	25	25	25	24	Adovnibezek
25 Ազան	26	26	26	25	Azan
26 Ակրաբիմ	27	27	27	26	Akrabim
27 Անաթովթ	28	28	28	27	Anat'ovt'
28 Արուէլ	29 Արուէր	29 Արուէր	29	28 Արուէր	Aruēl (VL Aruēr)
29 Աւովդ	30 Արոդ	30 Արոդ	30	29	Awovd (Abod)
30 Աննա	31	31	31	30	Anna
	32 Ասկարոն	32 Ասկարոն	32		(Askał n)
31 Ազովտոս	33	33	33	31	Azovtos
32 Ասկաղովն	34	34	34	32	Askałovn
33 Ակկարովն	35	35	35	33	Akkarovn
34 Արիմմաթեմ			36		Arimmat'em
				34 Ակկարոն	(Akkaron)
35 Աքերովք	36 Աբերովթ	36 Ասեբովթ	37	35	Ak'erovk' (VL Ak'er-ovt')
36 Աքիմելեք	37	37		36	Ak'imelek'

37 Աբիաթար					37	Abiat'ar
38 Ամատառա	38	38	38		38	Amattara
39 Աբիգեա	39	39 Աշիթեա	39		39	Abigea (VL Abit'ea)
40 Անրւս	40 Արւս	40 Արւս	40		40	Ank'us (VL Ak'us)
						(Abia)
41 Այենդովր	41 Այենովր	41 Այենովգ	41 Արուս		41	Ayendovr (VLL Ayenovd Ayenovg)
42 Աբեսողովմ	42	42	42 Աբիա		42	Abesałovm
43 Աբիտոփել	43	43	43 Այենովք		43	Ak'itop'el
44 Աբիմաաս	44	44	44		44	Ak'imaas
45 Աբեններ	45	45	45		45	Abenner
46 Ասաել	46	46	46		46	Asael
47 Ամեսսաի	47	47	47		47	Amessai
48 Աբենեզեր	48	48	48		48	Abenezer
49 Ասափ	49	49	49		49	Asap'
50 Ալելուիա	50 Ասին	50	50		50	Aleluia
						(Astin)

ONA I v C TYPE III : ORDER OF NAMES

No. 59		No. 62		
1	Ադամ	1		Adam
2	Ադային	2		Adayin
3	Ադադ	3		Adad
4	Ադդա	4		Adda
5	Ադին	5		Adin
6	Ադի	6		Adi
7	Ադոնիբեզեկ	7		Adonibezek
8	Ադոնա	8		Adona
9	Ադոնիա	9		Adonia
10	Ադոնիէլ	10		Adonīel
11	Ադդեր	11		Adder
12	Ադրազար	12		Adrazar
13	Ադրամելէք	13		Adramelēk'
14	Աբէղ	14		Abēł
15	Աբէղմայուզա	15		Abēlmayuza
16	Աբեղա	16		Abeła
17	Աբենէր	17		Abenēr
18	Աբենեզեր	18	Աբենեզ	Abenezer (VL Abenez)
19	Աբեդդար	19		Abeddar
20	Աբէլփի			Abēlp'i
21	Աբրամ	21		Abram
22	Աբրաամ	22		Abraam
23	Աբրոկ	23		Abrok
24	Աբիմելէք	24		Abimelēk'
25	Աբիթան	25		Abit'an
26	Աբիաթար	26		Abiat'ar
27	Աբիգեայ	27		Abigea
28	Աբիսողոմ	28		Abisołom
29	Աբիսակ	29		Abisak
30	Աբբիայ	30		Abbia
31	Աբբանայ	31		Abbana
32	Աբբա	32	Աբբիայ	Abba (VL Abbia)
		33	Աբբայէլ	(Abbayēl)
33	Աբանա	34		Abana
34	Աբաբովթ	35		Ababovt'

35	Աբիոն	36	Abion
36	Աբիւրիմ	37	Abiurim
37	Աբիուդ	38	Abiud
38	Աբդիու	39	Abdiu
39	Աբոտ	40	Abot
40	Ագար	41	Agar
41	Ագաբոս	42	Agabos
42	Ագռամբովն	43	Agṙambovn
43	Ագագ	44	Agag
44	Արփաքսաթ	45	Arp'ak'sat'
45	Արաբովթ	46	Arabovt'
46	Արամ	47	Aram
47	Արամաթի	48	Aramat'i
48	Արաբիայ	49	Arabia
49	Արա	50	Ara
50	Արրա		Arra

No. 64

1	Աբբա	35	Ագազ
2	Աբբանայ	36	Ագաութիւնք
3	Աբբոր	37	Ագարսա
4	Աբբայէլ	38	Ագապոս
5	Աբենէր	39	Ագդէն
6	Աբբոկ	40	Ագորանք
7	Աբդլմսիհ	41	Ագոն
8	Աբդիու	42	Ագուո
9	Աբեղա	43	Ագունիա
10	Աբբեթդարա	44	Ագոո
11	Աբեղբի	45	Ագովր
12	Աբենեզէր	46	Ադամ
13	Աբէլ	47	Ադադ
14	Աբէլմաուլայ	48	Ադդէր
15	Աբինն	49	Ադդա
16	Աբիմելէք	50	Ադին
17	Աբիդան		
18	Աբիդար		
19	Աբիդա		
20	Աբիսողոմ		
21	Աբիա		
22	Աբիուրիմ		
23	Աբիութ		
24	Աբող		
25	Աբրայ		
26	Աբրամ		
27	Աբրաամ		
28	Աբրաթ		
29	Ագապէն		
30	Ագապ		
31	Ագաթանգեղոս		
32	Ագարակբ		
33	Ագաթեմովթ		
34	Ագանել		

1	Abba	35	Agaǵ
2	Abbana	36	Agasut'iwnk'
3	Abbor	37	Agarsa
4	Abbayēl	38	Agabos
5	Abenēr	39	Agdēn
6	Abbok	40	Agorank'
7	Abdlmsih	41	Agon
8	Abdiu	42	Aguŕ
9	Abeła	43	Agunia
10	Abbedt'ara	44	Agoŕ
11	Abełbi	45	Agovr
12	Abenezēr	46	Adam
13	Abēł	47	Adad
14	Abēlmaula	48	Addēr
15	Abion	49	Adda
16	Abimelēk'	50	Adin
17	Abidan		
18	Abidar		
19	Abida		
20	Abisołom		
21	Abia		
22	Abiurim		
23	Abiut'		
24	Abod		
25	Abra		
26	Abram		
27	Abraam		
28	Abrat'		
29	Agapēn		
30	Agap		
31	Agat'angełos		
32	Agarakk'		
33	Agat'ŕemovt'		
34	Aganel		

No. 53

1A	{ Աբաքով[թ}	34	Ադդեր
1	Աբանայ	35	Ադի
2	Աբբայ	35	{Ադէն}
3	Աբբանայ	36	Ադին
4	Աբբայէլ	37	Ադին
4A	{Աբբէդ }	38	Ադ{դ}ին
5	Աբբիա	39	Ադին
6	Աբդիու	40	Ադոնիբեզեկ
7	Աբեդդար{այ }	41	Ադովնայ
8	Աբեդայ	42	Ադովնիայ
9	Աբէդ	43	Ադովնիէլ
10	Աբէդբի	44	Ադրայագար
11	Աբէդմայուդայ	45	Ադրամելէբ
12	Աբենեզեր	46	Ագագայէլ
13	Աբեննէր	47	Ագայէլ
14	Աբէսողոմ	48	Ագան
15	Աբիաթար	49	Ագապարայ
16	Աբիայ	50	Ագար
17	Աբիդեա		
18	Աբիթան		
19	Աբիմեդէբ		
20	Աբինն		
21	Աբիուդ		
22	Աբիուրիմ		
23	Աբիսակ		
24	Աբոտ		
25	Աբրաճամ		
26	Աբրաթ		
27	Աբրամ		
27A	{Աբրոկ}		
28	Ագաբոս		
29	Ագագ		
30	Ագաբրամ[թովն		
31	Ագար		
32	Ադամ		
33	Ադդա		

1A {Ababovt'}

1   Abana

2   Abba

3   Abbana

4   Abbayēl

4A {Abbēł}

5   Abbia

6   Abdiu

7   Abeddar{a}

8   Abeła

9   Abēł

10 Abēłbi

11 Abēłmayuła

12 Abenezer

13 Abennēr

14 Abēsołom

15 Abiat'ar

16 Abia

17 Abidea

18 Abit'an

19 Abimełek'

20 Abion

21 Abiud

22 Abiurim

23 Abisak

24 Abot

25 Abraham

26 Abrat'

27 Abram

27A {Abrok}

28 Agabos

29 Agag

30 Agabŕamt'ovn

31 Agar

32 Adam

33 Adda

34 Addēr

35 Adi

35A {Adēn}

36 Adin

37 Adin

38 Ad{d}in

39 Adin

40 Adonibezak

41 Adovna

42 Adovnia

43 Adovniēl

44 Adrayazar

45 Adramelēk'

46 Azazayēl

47 Azayēl

48 Azan

49 Azapara

50 Azar

ONA I v F TYPE VI : ORDER OF NAMES

No. 84   No. 84

 1 Ադամ   36 Արոտ
 2 Ադին   37 Աբրամ
 3 Ադոնիբեզեկ   38 Աբրաամ
 4 Ադոնիրամ   39 Աբրայ
 5 Ադոնա   40 Աբրոկ
 6 Ադոնիէլ   41 Ազար
 7 Ադոնիայ   42 Ազատմթովն
 8 Ադադ   43 Ազարոս
 9 Ադդայ   44 Ազովր
10 Ադդեր   45 Ազան
11 Ադրամէլիք   46 Ազայէլ
12 Ադրայագար   47 Ազազայէլ
13 Աբբա   48 Ազար
14 Աբբիայ   49 Ազարիայ
15 Աբբանայ   50 [   ]
16 Աբբայէլ
17 Արանայ
18 Արաբովթ
19 Արդիու
20 Արանէր
21 Աբենեզեր
22 Աբելմայուսայ
23 Աբեղդար
24 Աբեղայ
25 Աբէլ
26 Աբէսողոմ
27 Աբէլբի
28 Աբիաթր
29 Աբիգեայ
30 Աբիթան
31 Աբիմէլէք
32 Աբինն
33 Աբիուղ
34 Աբիուրիմ
35 Աբիսակ

1	Adam	36	Abot
2	Adin	37	Abram
3	Adonibezek	38	Abraam
4	Adoniram	39	Abra
5	Adona	40	Abrok
6	Adoniēl	41	Agar
7	Adonia	42	Agaŕmt'ovn
8	Adad	43	Agabos
9	Adda	44	Agovr
10	Adder	45	Azan
11	Adramēlik'	46	Azayēl
12	Adrayazar	47	Azazayēl
13	Abba	48	Azar
14	Abbia	49	Azaria
15	Abbana	50	[ ]
16	Abbayēl		
17	Abana		
18	Ababovt'		
19	Abdiu		
20	Abanēr		
21	Abenezer		
22	Abelmayusa		
23	Abeddar		
24	Abeła		
25	Abēl		
26	Abēsołom		
27	Abēlbi		
28	Abiat'ar		
29	Abigea		
30	Abit'an		
31	Abimēlēk'		
32	Abion		
33	Abiud		
34	Abiurim		
35	Abisak		

III

ONA   III

Յետրայեցւոց բանից մնացեալբ են բանզի յառաջագոյն ոչ

ունեցաք ի մտի շարադրել ընդ նմին բանի:

1	Աբբայ.	Հայր, ասրւոց է բառս:
2	Աբարիմ.	անցք կամ անցանողք:
3	Աբդեմելեք.	ծառայ թագաւորի:
4	Աբդենագո.	ծառայ պայծառութեան:
5	Աբդիաս.	ծառայ տեառն:
6	Աբդոն.	ծառայ:
7	Աբեդ.	ի ծնն ալիֆի, Հնձման քաղաք. իսկ ի ծնն Հէի ներ սկզբան, ունայնութիւն, որդի Աղամայ: Այս ըստ ղաղմատացւոց, իսկ ի մերս,
8	Աբէդ.	յաստուծոյ տուեալ մարգարէութիւն կամ տեսանելի կամ գլորշի սգոյ կամ գութ վերամբերեալ կամ երկիր պաղպեր:
9	Աբէսաղոմ.	Հայր խաղաղութեան:
10	Աբիա.	Հայր տեառն:
11	Աբիաթար.	Հայր բարձրացոյ:
12	Աբիգայիլ.	Հայր գնծութեան:
13	Աբիգայ.	Հոր իմոյ յայտնութիւն:
14	Աբիմելէք.	Հայր թագաւոր կամ Հոր իմոյ արքայու-թիւն:
15	Ամինադաբ.	Հայր Հարսանեաց:

(These) are those remaining of the Hebrew Words, for

previously we did not intend to arrange them with the

same vocabulary.

1	Abbay,	father, this is a Syriac word.
2	Abarim,	passage, or passers.
3	Abdemelek',	servant of king.
4	Abdenagō,	servant of brilliance.
5	Abdias,	servant of lord.
6	Abdōn,	servant.
7	Abel,	with Alif, city of wailing; but with Hē at the beginning, nothingness, son of Adam. This is according to the Dalmatians, but in our (tradition),
8	Abel.	prophecy given by God or visible or vapour of mourning or elevated pity or fruitful earth.
9	Abēsaɫom,	father of peace.
10	Abia,	father of lord.
11	Abiat'ar,	sublime father.
12	Abigayil,	father of rejoicing.
13	Abika,	my father's revelation.
14	Abimelēk',	father king or my father's kingdom.
15	Aminadab,	father of wedding.

16   Աբիսակ.   հոր տգիտութիւն կամ հոր իմոյ

                            աւետիք:

17   Աբներ.   հոր ճրագ:

18   Աբեներ.   հայր կամ որդի ճրագ{ի}:

19   Աբրա.   աղախին, յունաց է բառ:

20   Աբրամ.   հայր վերամբարձ կամ մեծարգոյ:

1   Աբբա | աստրոց} սիրացւոց | բառ   2 անցաւորք
3   Արղեմեղեք   4 Արղենագով | ծառա   5 Աբիղաս
7   Աբէղ | ի ծեռն 1°---իսկ} om | հէի} + որ է
Հաբէղ | սկզբանն | այս---մերս} om   8 om
9   Աբիսաղոմ   13 Աբիգաւղ   14 Աբիմեղեք |
կամ հոր իմոյ արքայութիւն} om   15 հարսանաւոր
16   Աբիսագ | կամ---աւետիք} om   17 Աբնէր
18   om   19 յունական   20 կամ մեծարգոյ} om

16 Abisak,   father's ignorance or my father's

                        gospel.

17 Abner,   father's candle.

18 Abener,   candle's father or son.

19 Abra,   maid-servant, it is a Greek word.

20 Abram,   exalted or revered father.

ln 1 MS 9 ln 2: Ona V ln 2: MS 9 is that whose text
       is printed by Wutz.

ln 2 MS 9 ln 1, Ona V ln 3.

ln 3 MS 9 ln 4, Ona V ln 5.

ln 4 MS 9 ln 3, Ona V ln 8.

ln 5 MS 9 ln 15: The form in MS 9 is somewhat corrupt,
       Աբիզաս "Abidas", and has, secondarily been
       placed lower in the alphabetical order. Ona V
       ln 4 has "Abdiu" with this etymology.

ln 6 MS 9 ln 6, Ona V ln 6.

ln 7 The words: with "Alif" city of weeping, but, are
       omitted by MS 9 ln 9. This etymology is clearly
       behind that of Ona V ln 9. See also Ona V ln 10.

       The introduction of "our tradition" for the etymo-
       logy of Abel is the insertion of the entry for
       Abel from Ona I (see Ona I, iv, ln 2, supra).
       This is not reflected in MS 9 or in Ona V.
       "Dalmatians" here designates the Latins.

ln 9 MS 9 ln 18, Ona V ln 12.

ln 10 MS 9 ln 10, Ona V ln 13.

ln 11 MS 9 ln 11, Ona V ln 14 different wording.

ln 12 MS 9 ln 12. In Ona V ln 14 the same etymology
       occurs with the name "Abigea".

ln 13 The form "Abigal" of MS 9 ln 13 seems preferable.
       Omitted by Ona V.

ln 14 MS 9 ln 16, Ona V ln 19: The second of the two
       etymologies does not occur in either of these
       sources. It is drawn from Ona I ln 11.

ln 15   Cf. MS 9 ln 19.   Contrast Ona V ln 17 and
         note there.

ln 16   MS 9 ln 17, Ona V ln 19.   The second meaning
         is to be found in Ona II ln 11.

lns 17-18 MS 9 ln 19 = ln 17.   MS 9 omits ln 18.   In
         Ona V ln 11 we read "Abenner, father's candle".
         Ln 18 corresponds to Ona I ln 51.

ln 19   MS 9 ln 21, Ona V ln 20.

ln 20   MS 9 ln 22, Ona V ln 22.   "And revered"   occurs
         in Ona I ln 6.

IV

ONA IV

Այլ բառ եբրայեցւոց է ի վերայ այբուբենից ըստ

անուանակոչութեանց.

1 (1)   (Ա)դամ.   երկիր կամ կոյս:

2 (2)   Աբէլ.   Աստուծոյ սրւեալ մարգարէութիւն:

3 (4)   Արփաքսադ.   մաքրութիւն տեսանելի:

4 (7)   Աբրահամ.   հայր ազգաց:

5 (11)   Աբիմելէք,   հոր իմոյ արքայութիւն:

6 (16)   Ամինադաբ.   ազգ ցանկալի:

7 (19)   Ահարոն.   ահա լեառն կամ հոգի կամ

                             բան:

8 (28)   Ամուրհացիք.   չեղեալ կամ ծաղեալ:

9 (29)   Ամադէկ.   ազգ լեզուող:

10 (33) Անաբովթ.   պատասխանի:

11 (36) Աննայ.   արարած նորայ:

12 (48) Աքիսողմ.   հայր խաղաղութեան:

13 (40) Արիմաթեմ.   բարձրութիւնք կամ լերինք:

14 (49) Ակիտաբէլ.   եղբօր գլորուն:

15 (56) Ալէլուիայ.   աւհ́նեցէք զտէր կամ գովեցէք զաս-
                                                        տուած:

16 (60) Ամովսիայ.   յազգէ հալատարմէն:

17 (65) Ազագիէլ.   տեսիլ աստուծոյ:

18 (76) Աքազ.   զօրութիւն:

19 (72) Ասուր.   խորհ́ուրդ սուրբ:

20 (74) Ադոնա.   տէր:

21 (75) Ադոնիայ.   տերանց տէր:

Another vocabulary of the Hebrews is based upon the alphabet according to the names.

1 (1)   Adam,   earth or virgin.

2 (2)   Abēl   prophecy given from God.

3 (4)   Arp'ak'sad, visible cleanliness.

4 (7)   Abraham   father of nations.

5 (11) Abimelēk',   my father's kingdom.

6 (16) Aminadab,   desirable nation.

7 (19) Aharon,   behold a mountain or a spirit or a
                     word.

8 (28) Amurhac'ik', not having been or having mocked.

9 (29) Amałek,   licking nation.

10 (33) Anabovt',   answer.

11 (36) Anna,   his (her) creation.

12 (48) Abisolom,   father of peace.

13 (40) Arimat'em,   elevations or mountains.

14 (49) Akidabēl,   brother's ruin.

15 (56) Alēluia,   bless the Lord or praise God.

16 (60) Amovsia,   from the faithful people.

17 (65) Azaziēl,   vision of God.

18 (76) Akaaz,   power.

19 (72) Asur,   holy thought.

20 (74) Adona,   Lord.

21 (75) Adonia,   Lord of lords.

22 (78) Անանիայ. շնորհք:

23 (79) Ազարիայ. արձակումն:

24 (82) Աւզոստոս. տոն ոգի ստացանք:

25 (85) Անդրիաս. ազգի սիրելի կամ վայելուչ:

26 (87) Ամէն. եղիցի կամ ճշմարտութիւն:

27 (93) Աբբա. հայր հոր:

28 (69) Ամբակում. հայր յարուցանող կամ արդարացեալ:

29 (23) Առած. պատգամ.

30 (60) Ամասիայ. յազգէ հաւատարիմ:

31 (էջ 864) Ազբակ. մուկ:

32 արգաւանդ. երկիր բերող կամ պարարտ:

33 արգ<ա>սաւոր. գործեալ:

34 արդարեւ. է այսպէս:

35 արւարծան. ոտար կամ այլազգի:

36 անուրջ. ծածուկ կամ երազ:

37 անընդհատ. միակարգ կամ ստէպ ստէպ:

38 անշրպետ. անշատող:

39 առհաւատչեա. գրաւական ազգական:

40 ապաշաւիլ. փոշեմանիլ:

41 անդրադարձումն. յետ դառնալ կամ երկու

դիմաց կարդալ. որ է

այսպէս սողոս:

22 (78) Anania ,   grace.

23 (79) Azaria,   deliverance.

24 (82) Awgōstos,   we received a feast soul

                      (<u>corr. for</u> celebrating).

25 (85) Andrias,   of a beloved nation or delightful.

26 (87) Amēn,   let it be or truth.

27 (93) Abba,   father's father.

28 (69) Ambakum,   resurrecting father or righteous.

29 (23) Aṙac,   command.

30 (60) Amasia,   from a faithful people.

31(p.864n) Agbak,   mouse.

32   <u>arqawand</u>,   fruitful earth or rich.

33   <u>arq⟨a⟩sawor</u>, praised.

34   <u>ardarew</u>,   it is thus.

35   <u>aruarjan</u>,   strange or alien.

36   <u>anurǰ</u>.   secret or quick.

37   <u>anəndhat</u>,   of single order or very often.

38   <u>anǰrpet</u>,   separator.

39   <u>aṙhawatč'ea</u>, pledge, relative.

40   <u>apašawil</u>,   repent.

41   <u>andradarjumn</u>, to turn back or to set in two

                      directions.

                      which is thus ⌐<u>unknown word</u>⌐.

42 (130) Բաբելոն.   փոփոխումն կամ խռովութիւն:

43 (134) Բենիամին.   որդի վշտաց կամ սգոյ:

44 (173) Բեթսաիրայ.   տուն ողորմութեան:

45 (168) Բէլ.   այլապիսի աստուած:

46 (182) Բելիար.   ապատամբ:

47 (167) Բոսոր.   կարմրութիւն մարմնոց:

48 (141) Բեսելիէլ.   ի հովանի աստուծոյ:

49 (139) Բերսաբէ.   դուստր լցեալ կամ զօրաւոր:

50 (169) Բադտասար.   անդտութիւն երանութեան:

51 (171) Բարդուղիմէոս.   որդիք սատյք աստուծոյ:

52 (173) Բեդասայիրայ.   տուն ողորմութեան:

53 (176) Բեղզեբուղ.   դեւ պարատու կամ իշխան

                            ճիւաց:

54 (177) Բառնաբաս.   որդի մխիթարութեան:

55 (153) Բաճադ.   պատրիճ:

56 (196) Բերովբա.   ճանճ:

57 (156) Բեթլէճեմ.   տուն ճացի կամ տուն մսի:

42	(130)	Babelon,	exchange or confusion.
43	(134)	Beniamin,	son of pains or of sorrow.
44	(173)	Bet'saida,	house of mercy.
45	(160)	Bel,	different god.
46	(182)	Beliar,	rebellion.
47	(167)	Bosor,	redness of bodies.
48	(141)	Beseliel,	in the shade of God.
49	(139)	Bersabē,	full daughter or powerful.
50	(169)	Baltasar,	undeceitfulness of benediction.
51	(171)	Baldulimēos,	assured sons of God.
52	(173)	Bedsayida,	house of mercy.
53	(176)	Belzebul,	inclusive demon or prince of demons.
54	(177)	Barnabas,	son of pity.
55	(153)	Bahal,	seducer.
56	(196)	Bcrovba,	fly.
57	(156)	Bet'lēhem,	house of bread or house of meat.

V

ONA V

300բ 1   Մեկնութիւն անուանց յեբրայեցւոց

                լեզուէ ի հայ բարբառ

Աբբայ.	Հայր ասորց է բառ:
Աբբարիմ.	անցք կամ անցoրք:
Արդիու.	ծառայ տեառն:
5 Արդիմելեք.	ծառայ արքայի:
Արդոն.	ծառայ:
Աբեդդար.	ծառայ մարդոյ:
Աբեդնագով.	ծառայ պայծառութեան:
Աբէլ.	սուգ կամ լալումն կամ քաղաք:
10 Աբէլ.	ունայնութիւն որդի ադամայ:
Աբեններ.	հոր ճրագ:
Աբէսոդոմ.	հայր խաղաղութեան:
Աբիայ.	հայր տեառն:
Աբիաթար.	հայր գերագոյն:
15 Աբիգեա.	հայր գնծութեան:
Աբիմելեք.	հայր թագաւոր:
Աբինադաբ.	հայր կամաւոր:
Աբեսսեա.	ցամաք կամ տրտմութիւն:
Աբիսակ.	հոր անգիտութիւն.
20 Աբրա.	ադախին յունաց է բառ:
Աբրաամ.	հայր բազմութեան:
Աբրամ.	հայր վերամբարձ:
Ազաք.	մարախ:
Ազազ.	տանիս:

300v 1   Interpretation of Names from the Hebrew

              Tongue into the Armenian Language

Abba,	father, it is a Syriac word.
Abbarim,	passage or passers.
Abdiu,	servant of lord.
5 Abdimelēk',	servant of king.
Abdon,	servant.
Abeddar,	servant of man.
Abednagov,	servant of brilliance.
Abēl,	mourning, or weeping, or city.
10 Abēl,	nothingness, son of Adam.
Abenner,	father's candle.
Abēsolom,	father of peace.
Abia,	father of lord.
Abiat'ar,	sublime father.
15 Abigea,	father of rejoicing.
Abimēlēk',	father king.
Abinadab,	willing father.
Abessea,	dry land, or sadness.
Abisak,	father's ignorance.
20 Abra,	maid-servant, it is a Greek word.
Abraam,	father of multitude.
Abram,	exalted father.
Agab,	locust.
Agag,	roof.

25 Ազան.   նեղութիւն:/

301ա   Ազար.   պանդուխտ:

       Ադամ.   մարդ երկրային կամ կարմիր:

       Ադոնա.   տէր:

       Ադոնայի.   տեարք իմ:

30 Ադունիա.   տիրող կամ տէր:

       Ազարիա.   օգնութիւն տեառն:

       Ագոմտոս.   կոդոպուտ:

       Ագովր.   օգնական:

       Աթադիա.   ժամանակ տեառն:

35 Ակկարոն.   ամլութիւն:

       Աճարոն.   լեառն կամ լեռնային:

       Աճովտ.   գովասանող:

       Ադեղուիայ.   աւրճնեցէք զտէր:

       Ադեկսանդեր.   քաջ օգնական:

40 Ադեկսանդրիայ.   եբրա<յերէն> նոյ որ է ճուն:

       Ամադեք.   թագաւոր:

       Ամամ.   մայր կամ երկիւղ նոցա:

       Աման.   խռովեցուցանող:

       Ամանայ.   ճաւատ կամ ճշմարտութիւն:

45 Ամբակում.   ողբասէր:

       Ամրի.   դառն կամ զօր այն կամ
                      տերութիւն:

       Ամասիա.   քաջ կամ զօրեղ:

       Ամեսայի.   ժողովրդեան պարգեւ:

25	Agan,	affliction./
301r	Agar,	sojourner.
	Adam,	earthly man, or red.
	Adona,	lord.
	Adonayi,	my lords.
30	Adonia,	ruler or lord.
	Azaria,	lord's help.
	Azovtcs,	booty.
	Azovr,	helpful.
	At'ałia,	lord's time.
35	Akkaron,	sterility.
	Aharon,	mountain, or mountainous.
	Ahovt,	praiser.
	Ałēłuia,	praise the Lord.
	Ałeksandēr,	brave, helpful.
40	Ałeksantria,	Hebr<cw> Noy which is cruel.
	Amałēk',	king.
	Amam,	mother, or their fear.
	Aman,	disturber.
	Amana,	faith, or truth.
45	Ambakum,	love of laments.
	Amri,	bitter, or that force, or
		mastery.
	Amasia,	brave, or powerful.
	Amesayi,	people's gift.

Ամէն.   եղիցի կամ հաստատուն լիցի:

50 Ամինադաբ.   ժողովուրդ կամաւոր:
   Ամմոն.   ժողովուրդ նորա:
   Ամոն.   հաւատարիմ:
   Ամովս.   զօրեղ կամ բաշ կամ հայրն /
301բ   եսայեա է:

   Ամովս.   ծանրացեալ, մարգարէն
                       է:

55 Ամուրհացի.   դառն կամ ապստամբ:
   Անանիա.   ամպ տեառն:
   Անաթովթ.   պատասխանի կամ երգ:
   Անզէաս.   ուրախարար:
   Անդրէաս.   քաշագոյն:
60 Աննա.   ցանկալի կամ ողորմած:
   Անտիոքիա.   կառք:
   Ապողոս.   ճարտար կամ խորհրդական:
   Ասեր.   որդի յակոբայ աւրհնութիւն կամ
                       երանութիւն:

   Ասթինէ.   րմպող:
65 Ասուր.   որգայթ վերանող կամ երանելի:
   Ասվերուս.   իշխան կամ գլուխ:
   Ատարովթ.   հօտք կամ ստացուածք:
   Ասքա.   զարդարեալ:

	Amēn,	let it be, or let it be estab-
		lished.
50	Aminadab,	willing people.
	Ammon,	his people.
	Amon,	faithful.
301v	Amovs,	powerful, or brave, or the
		father/of Isaiah.
	Amovs,	having become heavy, it is the
		prophet.
55	Amurhac'i,	bitter, or rebellion.
	Anania,	lord's cloud.
	Anat'ovt',	reply, or song.
	Angēas,	joyous.
	Andrēas,	most brave.
60	Anna,	desirable, or merciful.
	Antiok'ia,	chariot.
	Apolos,	skillful or mysterious.
	Aser,	son of Jacob; blessing or
		felicity.
	Ast'inē,	drinker.
65	Asur,	ambush, ascender, or felicitous.
	Asverus,	ruler, or head.
	Astarovt,	flocks, or possessions.
	Ask'a,	having decorated.

Արաքացիք.   երեկեանք:

70 Արաքացիք.   երրայեցերէն սաքայ որ է դար-
                                ձումն:

Արամ.   բարձրութիւն:

Արարատ.   անէծք դողունեան:

Արբոկ.   չորք:

Արի ‹ո ›պագոս.   բլուր մարտի:

75 Արոն.   տապանակ կամ երգ:

Արտաքսեր‹ ք ›սէս. ծառագայթ կամ անէծք:

Արփաքսաթ.   բժշկող:

302բ Աքայեաք.   եղբայր / ՞որ:

Աքիմելէք.   եղբայր իմ արքայ:

80 Աքայիա.   վիշտ կամ նեղութիւն:

Աքազ.   ընբռնող կամ ստացող:

Աքիտոփէլ.   եղբայր բարութեան:

Բաբէլ.   խառնակութիւն կամ ամօթ:

Բաթուէլ.   որդի աստուծոյ:

85 ԲաՀադ.   կունք կամ տիրող:

Բ‹ ըլլա.   նաժիշտ ռաքելա

                  ծերացեալ կամ զարՀուրեալ:

Բաղամ.   Հնութիւն ժողովրդեան:

Բաղակ.   աւերող:

Բալլա.   քաղաք ընկլուզող կամ աւերող:

90 Բանեա.   որդի տեառն:

Բաներեգէս.   որդիք որոտման:

	Arabac'ik',	belonging to yesterday.
70	Arabac'ik',	Hebrew Sabay, which is return.
	Aram,	height.
	Ararat,	curses of trembling.
	Arbok,	four.
	Ari⟨o⟩pagos,	hill of battle.
75	Aron,	ark, or song.
	Ardak'ser⟨k'⟩sēs,	ray, or curse.
	Arp'ak'sat',	healer.
	Ak'ayeab,	father's/brother.
	Ak'imelēk',	my brother king.
80	Ak'ayia,	sorrow, or affliction.
	Ak'az,	seizer, or possessor.
	Ak'itop'ēl,	brother of goodness.
	Babēl,	confusion, or shame.
	Bat'uel,	son of God.
85	Bahaɫ,	idol or master.
	Balla,	Rachel's maid-servant;
		aged, or amazed.
	Baɫaam,	people's antiquity.
	Baɫak,	destroyer.
	Balla,	city, swallower, or destroyer.
90	Banea,	lord's son.
	Banereges,	thunder's sons.

302r

	Բատոս.	շափ հալողականաց:
	Բարակ.	փայլակն:
	Բարիովնա.	որդի աղաւնոյ:
95	Բարսաբայ.	որդի դարձման:
	Բառնաբաս.	որդի մխիթարութեան:
	Բարուք.	աւրհնեալ:
	Բարտիմէոս.	որդի կոյր:
	Բէելզեբուղ.	կուռք ճանճիկ:
100	Բեզեկ.	փայլակն կամ խիստ:
	Բեթանիա.	տուն հնազանդութեան կամ
		նեղութեան:
	Բեթաբաթայ.	տուն անցից:
302բ	Բեթաւան./	տուն ունայնութեան:
	Բեթէլ.	տուն աստուծոյ:
105	Բեթէր.	բաժանումն:
	Բեթղահէմ.	տուն հացի:
	Բերսաբէ.	դուստր երդման:
	Բեթսաբէէ.	տուն երդման:
	Բեթսամիւս.	տուն արեգական:
110	Բեթսայիդայ.	տուն պտղոց.
	Բեթքաբէ.	տուն բերանոյ հովտաց:
	Բեթքարովր.	տուն անդնդոց:
	Բելիար.	նենգաւոր կամ առանց լծոյ:
	Բելփեքրովր.	կուռք անդնդոց:

	Batos,	measure of liquids.
	Barak,	ray.
	Bariovna,	dove's son.
95	Barsaba,	son of return.
	Barnabas,	son of mercy.
	Baruk',	blessed.
	Bartimēos,	blind son.
	Bēelzebuł,	idol fly.
100	Bezek,	ray, or difficult.
	Bet'ania,	house of obedience or of affliction.
	Bet'abat'a,	house of passings.✓
302v	Bet'awan,	house of inutility.
	Bet'ēl,	house of God.
105	Bet'er,	division.
	Bet'łahem,	house of bread.
	Bersabē,	oath's daughter.
	Bet'sabēē,	oath's house.
	Bet'samiws,	sun's house.
110	Bet'sayida,	house of fruit.
	Bet'bak'ē,	house of mouth of valley.
	Bet'bak'ovr,	house of abyss.
	Beliar,	treacherous, or without yoke
	Belp'ek'ovr,	idol of abyss.

115 Բեզմովթ.   խաշինք կամ շորքոտանիք:

Բենիամին.   որդի աջոյ:

Բեննի.   որդի վշտաց իմոց:

Բետուլ.   կոյս:

Բերա.   շրհոր:

120 Բերսաբէէ.   շրհոր երդման:

Բեթդագոն.   տուն ցորենւոյ:

Բէլ.   հնացեալ:

Բելա.   ընկլուզող կամ աւերող:

Բոյոս.   ի զորութեան:

125 Բոսվր.   ամրութիւն:

Բրեսիթ.   առաջին գիրք օրինաց

                  այսպէս անուանի:

Գաբայեա.   բլուր:

Գաբայադ.   ընկեցումն: /

303ա Գաբրիէլ.   այր աստուած կամ աստուծոյ:

130 Գաթ.   երանելի կամ արագահաս:

Գաղգաղ.   երանութիւն երանութեան կամ

                  արագ գործդ:

Գագեր.   հատանումն:

Գալիլեա.   հոլովական:

Գաղատացիք.   կաթեալք:

115	Behmovt',	sheep, or quadrupeds.
	Beniamin,	son of right hand.
	Benoni,	son of my affliction.
	Betul,	virgin.
	Bera,	well.
120	Bersabēē,	well of oath.
	Bet'dagon,	house of corn.
	Bēl,	aged.
	Bela,	swallower, or destroyer.
	Boyos,	in power.
125	Bosovr,	strength.
	Bresit',	The first book of the Law is named thus.
	Gabayea,	hill.
	Gabayad,	a casting./
303r	Gabriēl,	man God or of God.
130	Gat',	felicitous, or arriving quickly.
	Gadgad,	felicity of felicity, or quickly powerful.
	Gazer,	cutting.
	Galilea,	circular.
	Gaɫatac'ik',	those having dripped.

135 Գաղզաղայ.   անիւ կամ անդրադարձումն:

    Գեթաղ.   սաՀման:

    Գեղեոն.   փշրող կամ կործանող:

    ԳեՀոն.   լանջիք.

    ԳեՀենին.   Հովիտ տրտմուԹեան:

140 Գերսմ.   պանդուխտ անդ:

    Գերսոն.

    Գոզ.   տանիս:

    Գողզոթայ.   կառափելոյ տեղի այս է ուր

                      զլուխս մեռելոց

                      դնին:
    Գողիաթ.   փոփոխումն
145 Գոմեր: շափ:

    Գոմորայ.   ժողովուրդ ապտամբ:

    Դաբրէիովմին.   բանք աւուրց կամ զիրք:

    Դագոն.   ցորեան:

    Դալիլա.   աղքատուԹիւն:

150 Դաթան.   արարողուԹիւն կամ օրէնք:

303բ Դամասկոս.   ցող արեան կամ նմանուԹիւն բղցոյ

                      կամ ձննդեան Հոգար/կուԹիւն:

    Դան.   դատող կամ դատաստան:

    Դանիէլ.   դատաստան աստուծոյ:

    ԴարեՀ.   խնդրող:

155 Դաւիթ.   սիրելի:

    Դեբովրա.   մեղուք կամ բան:

135	Galgalay,	wheel, or retrogression.
	Gebal,	limit.
	Gedēon,	crusher, or destroyer.
	Gehon,	lungs.
	Gehenin,	valley of sadness.
140	Gersom,	sojourner there.
	Gerson,	. . .
	Gog,	ceiling.
	Golgot'a,	place of execution, this is where the heads of the dead are placed.
145	Gomer,	measure.
	Gomoray,	people rebellion.
	Dabrēiovmin,	words of days, or a book.
	Dagon,	wheat.
	Dalila,	poverty.
150	Dat'an,	ceremony, or law.
303v	Damaskos,	dew of blood, or likeness of flame, or care of/birth.
	Dan,	judger, or judgement.
	Daniēl,	god's judgement.
	Dareh,	searcher.
155	Dawit',	beloved.
	Debovra,	bees, or word.

Դեկապոլիս. ժ. քաղաքաց:

Դիաբուլոս. ծորեալ:

Դիդիմոս.

160 Դիթալոսն. երկու ծովք:

Դինա. դատաստան կամ դատող:

Դիոնիսիոս. յատուծոյ ցորեալ յունաց
է բառ:

Դովեկ. տրտմեալ կամ
աշխատեալ:

Դովր. ծնունդ կամ լինելութիւն:

165 Դովրա. ծնունդ կամ բնակութիւն:

Եբադ. կոյտ Հնութեան:

Եբեր. ընկեր կամ Հաղորդակից կամ
անցք:

Եբրայեցի. անցաւոր:

Եզիպտոս. նեղուածք կամ անձկութիւն:

170 Եզդոմ. որթ:

Եղեմ. վայելչութին կամ փափկութիւն:

Եղոմ. կարմիր կամ երկրային:

Եզեկիա. զօրութիւն տեառն:

Եզեկիէլ. զօրութիւն աստուծոյ:

175 Եզրաս. օգնական կամ զաւիթ:

Եզրիէլ. օգնութիւն աստուծոյ:/

Dekapōlis,	of ten cities.
Diabolos,	having flowed
Didimos	. . .
160 Dit'alason,	two seas.
Dina,	judgement, or judger.
Dionisios,	bedewed by God; it is a Greek word.
Dovek,	saddened, or having laboured.
Dovr,	birth, or generation.
165 Dovra,	birth, or dwelling.
Ebaɫ,	heap (or: meadow) of antiquity.
Eber,	friend, or participating, or passage.
Ebrayec'i,	one who passes.
Egiptos,	afflictions, or narrowness.
170 Egɫom,	calf.
Edem,	enjoyment, or delight.
Edom,	red, or earthly.
Ezekia,	lord' power.
Ezekiēl,	god's power.
175 Ezras,	helpful, or portico.
Ezriēl,	God's help./

304ա   Եզրով.   նետ գնծուβեան :

           Եβամ.   բաշուβիւն նոցա :

           Եβովպիա.   յունարէն շերմուβիւն եւ եբրայե-
                                  ցերէն սեւուβիւն կամ սեաւ :

180   Ելզանայ.   աստուած նախանծոտ :

           Ելքանան.   աստուծոյ շնորհք կամ ողորմուβիւն :

           Եղիա.   աստուած տէր :

           Եղիակիմ.   աստուծոյ յարուβիւն :

           Եղիազար.   աստուծոյ օգնուβիւն :

185   Եղիմելէք.   աստուած իմ արքայ :

           Եղինաβան.   աստուած ետ :

           Եղիշէ.   աստուծոյ փրկուβիւն կամ աստուած
                                            փրկիշ :

           Եղիսաբեβ.   աստուած երդման :

           Եկլեսիա ‹ս›տէս.   քարոզող :

190   Եմաւուս.   երկիւղած ի խորհրդոյ :

           Եմմանուէլ.   ընդ մեզ աստուած :

           Ենգենիա.   նաւակատիկ :

           Եննոն.   ահա նմա :

           Ենովս.   մարդ կամ այր :

195   Ենովք.   ունտեալ :

           Եսայիայ.   փրկուβիւն տեառն :

           Եսաւ.   առնող կամ գործող :

           Եսβեր.   ծածկեալ :

           Ելբուլոս.   ճարտար :

304r	Ezrov,	arrow of rejoicing.
	Et'am,	their bravery.
	Et'ovpia,	in Greek, warmth; and in Hebrew, blackness or black.
180	Elkana,	jealous god.
	Elk'anan,	god's grace or mercy.
	Elia,	god lord.
	Eliakim,	rising of god.
	Eliazar,	god's help.
185	Elimelēk',	my god king.
	Elinat'an,	god gave.
	Eliše,	god's salvation or god saviour.
	Elisabet',	god of oath.
	Eklesiastēs,	preacher
190	Emawus,	fearing counsel.
	Emmanuēl,	god (is) with us.
	Enkenia,	inauguration.
	Ennon,	behold for him.
	Enovs,	human being, or man.
195	Enovk',	having promised.
	Esayia,	lord's salvation.
	Esaw,	doer, or maker.
	Est'er,	hidden.
	Eubulos,	ingenious.

200 Երամէէ լ.   ողորմութիւն աստուծոյ:

     Երեմիա.   քարձրութիւն տեառն:

     Երիքով.   լուսին կամ ամիս:

     Երրւսադէմ.   տեսութիւն խադադութեան կամ
                                    տեսութիւն կատարեալ: /
304բ Ելա.   կենդանի:

205 Եփրա<թայ>.   առատութիւն կամ պտդաբեր:

     Եփրայիմ.   պտղաբեր կամ աճող:

     Եփրոն.   հող կամ մոխիր:

     Զաբուղուն.   բնակութիւն:

     Զամրի.   երգող:

210 Զարայ.   արեւելք:

     Զաքարիայ.   յիշատակ տեառն:

     Զաքէոս.   անարատ:

     Զեբեդեա.   օժտեալ:

     Զեբէէ.   պատարագ:

215 Զորաբաբէ լ.   ոտար յամoթոյ

     Էլլեսմովթ.   երկրորդ գիրք օրինաց:

     Թադէոս.   քարեքանoղ:

     Թամար.   տերեւ կամ ոստ:

     Թարայ.   անուշահոտ:

220 Թարսիս.   խորհրդագգածութիւն ուրախութեան:

     Թաւ.   նշան:

     Թափoր.   ընտրութիւն կամ մաքրութիւն:

     Թերաթիմ.   տիպք կամ կուռք:

200 Erameēl,   god's mercy.

Eremia,   lord's exaltation.

Erik'ov,   moon or month.

Erusalem,   vision of peace, or perfect vision⌿.

304v   Ewa,   living.

205 Ep'ra<t'a>,   abundance, or fruitful.

Ep'rayim,   fruitful, or increasing.

Ep'ron,   dust, or ashes.

Zabulun,   dwelling.

Zamri,   singer.

210 Zaray,   east.

Zak'aria,   lord's memorial.

Zak'ēos,   immaculate.

Zebedea,   having given.

Zebēe,   sacrifice.

215 Zorababēl,   strange to shame.

Ellēsmovt',   second book of the Law.

T'adēos,   praiser.

T'amar,   leaf or branch.

T'ara,   sweet-smelling.

220 T'arsis,   spiritual teaching of happiness.

T'aw,   sign.

T'ap'ōr,   election, or cleanliness.

T'erat'im,   likeness, or idol.

Թ <n> բէլ .   աշխարհի ստացուած :

225 Թովմաս .   անդունդք կամ խորք կամ կրկին :

      Թոփոթոր .   զանկակ կամ դարձութիւն :

      ի <եզրա̈>էլ .   զաւակ աստուծոյ :

      իթամար .   կղզի ոստոյ :

      իսահակ .   ծիծաղ :

230 իսաքար .   է վարձ կամ պարգեւ :

      իմայէլ .   լուր աստուծոյ : /

305ա իսրայէլ .   յաղթող աստուծոյ կամ տեսող
                                                          աստուծոյ :

      Լիա .   աշխատեալ կամ վաստակեալ :

      Լիբանոս .   պայծառ :

235 Լիբիա .   եբրայեցերէն լուբիմ այս է սիրտ

      Լիթոստրոտոս .   քարամբք շարժեալ յունաց   ծովու :

                                         է բառ :

      Խառան .   ուեներալ .

      Կադէս .   սրբութիւն :

      Կահաթ .   ժողով :

240 Կային .   ստացուած կամ ստացեալ :

      Կանա .   նախանձ կամ ՞ետեւումն :

      Կասթին   իբրեւ դեւք :

      Կարիաթարիմ .   քաղաք մայրեաց :

      Կարիաթսեփէր .   քաղաք նամակաց :

245 Կարկառ .   բլուր վկայութեան :

      Կարմէլ .   ծանուցումն թլփտութեան կամ զանն
                                                      Թլփատեալ :

T'obēl,   possession of world.

225 T'ovmas,   abyss, or depths, or double.

T'op'ot'or,   bell, or return.

I‹ezray›ēl, god's seed.

It'amar,   branch's island.

Isahak,   laughter.

230 Isak'ar,   is reward, or offering.

Ismayēl,   god's listening. /

305r Israyēl,   vanquisher of god, or seer of god.

Lia,   having toiled, or having laboured.

Libanos,   shining.

235 Libia,   Hebrew Lubim, that is heart of sea.

Lit'ostratos, moved by stones; it is a Greek
                 word.

Xaṙan,   destroyed.

Kadēs,   holiness.

Kahat',   gathering.

240 Kayin,   possession, or having possessed.

Kana,   envy or imitation.

Kast'in,   like demons.

Kariat'arim, city of forests.

Kariat'sep'ēr, city of letters.

245 Karkaṙ,   hill of witness.

Karmel,   declaration of circumcision, or
                 circumcised lamb.

	Կափանայում.	ազրակ ապաշխարութեան:
	Կեդար.	սեւութիւն կամ տրտմութիւն:
	Կեդրոն.	սեւեցեալ կամ տրտում:
250	Կերէաս.	ուրախ:
	Կեփաս.	պետրոս ի վիմէ:
	Կինովթ.	ողբք:
	Կիս.	խոշոր:
	Կղէոպաս.	փարք աստուծոյ:
255	Կիպրոս.	գեղեցիկ:
	Կիւրոս.	իբրեւ թշուառական: /
305բ	Կողոսացիք.	պաղատանք րդծից:
	Կորբան.	պարգեւ կամ ընծայ:
	Կորխա.	գոշոդ կամ կարդացոդ կամ կնդակ:
260	Հայաստան.	եբրայեցերէն արարադ որ է
		անէծք սասանութեան:
	Հերմոն.	աւերումն:
	Հելի.	ընծայ կամ պատարագ:
	Հելիպոդիս.	եբրայեցերէ ον որ է
		վիշտ:
	Հնդատա	եբրայեցերէն սոփեր որ է
		քաղաքացի:
265	Հնդիկք.	գովութիւն:
	Հոդեփենէս.	քաշ գօրագլուխ:
	Հոմ.	բարձր կամ վերամբարձ:

	Kap'aṙnayum,	village of penitence.
	Kedar,	blackness, or sadness.
	Kedron,	blackened, or sad.
250	Kerēas,	happy.
	Kep'as,	Petros, from rock.
	Kinovt',	lamentations.
	Kis,	rough.
	Kłeōpas,	glory of god.
255	Kipros,	beautiful.
	Kiwros,	as if miserable.
305v	Kołosac'ik',	supplications of prayers.
	Korban,	gift, or offering.
	Korxa,	caller, or reader, or bald.
260	Hayastan,	in Hebrew Ararat, which is curse of shaking.
	Hermon,	destruction.
	Heli,	offering, or sacrifice.
	Helipōlis,	in Hebrew On, which is affliction.
	Hndastan,	in Hebrew Sop'er, which is citizen.
265	Hndikk'	praise.
	Hołēp'eṙnēs,	brave general.
	Hṙom,	high, or exalted.

	Հորւթ.	լիացեալ:
	Ղաբան.	սպիտակ կամ պայծառ:
270	Ղազարոս.	աստուծոյ օգնուիթւն:
	Ղամէք.	աղքատ կամ խոնարհեալ:
	Ղապիդվթ.	փայլատակունք:
	Ղեկի.	օրէնք:
	Ղեւի.	շաղկապեալ:
275	Ղեքի.	կզակ:
	Ղեւիաթան.	շաղկապ կամ ընկերութիւն իւր:
	Ղովտ.	խառնեալ կամ պատեալ:
	Մայասիա.	գործ տեառն:
	Մատքեա.	կողոպտեալ:
306ա 280	Մաղիան./	դատաստան:
	Մաթուսաղայ.	զմահ իւր խնդրող:
	Մագդաղենացի.	մեծացեալ:
	Մակեդոն.	քրց:
	Մաղաքիայ.	հրեշտակ տեառն:
285	Մաղադէթ.	փառաբանող զաստուած
	Մաղքոս.	թագաւոր:
	Մամզէր.	ի պոռնկէ ծրնեալ:
	Մամոնայ.	մեծութիւն կամ ստացուած:
	Մանայեմ.	մխիթարիչ:
290	Մանասէ.	մոռացումն:
	Մանովէ.	հանգիստ:

		Hɫut',	filled.
		Ɫaban,	white, or brilliant.
	270	Ɫazaros,	god's help.
		Ɫamēk',	poor, or humbled.
		Ɫapiovt',	lightenings.
		Ɫeki,	law.
		Ɫewi,	joined.
	275	Ɫek'i,	chin.
		Ɫewiat'an,	junction, or his friendship.
		Ɫovt,	mixed, or surrounded.
		Mayasia,	lord's work.
		Maak'ea,	despoiled.
306r	280	Madian,/	judgement.
		Mat'usaɫa,	seeker of his death.
		Magdaɫenac'i,	having increased.
		Makedon,	flame.
		Maɫak'ia,	lord's angel.
	285	Maɫalēt',	praiser of God.
		Maɫk'os,	king.
		Mamzēr,	born of a prostitute.
		Mamona,	greatness, or possession.
		Manayem,	comforter.
	290	Manasē,	forgetfulness.
		Manovē,	rest.

Մառա.	*դառն.*
Մասադոթ.	*գիրք առակաց* *ասի:*
Մասեփա.	*պահապան:*
295 *Մասսա.*	*բեռն:*
Մաթէոս.	*պարգեւեալ:*
Մարթայ.	*կոչող:*
Մարիամ.	*բարձրացեալ կամ դառնութեան ձով:*
Մելքիա.	*թագաւոր տեառն:*
300 *Մելքիսեդէկ.*	*թագաւոր արդարութեան:*
Մելքիսուայ.	*թագաւոր փրկիչ:*
Մելքող.	*ով զամենայն:*
Մեմփիբոստէ.	*ի բերանոյ ամօթոյ:*
Մեսոդամ.	*Խադադարար*
305 *Մեսոպոտանիա.*	*միջագետ:*
Միսափաթ,	*որ է կաղէս դատաստան:*
Մեղքայ.	*արքայ:*
Միքա.	*աղքատ:*
Միքայէլ.	*ով իբրեւ զաստուած:*
310 *Միսիա.*	*զազիր: /*
306բ *Միքիա.*	*ով իբրեւ զտէր:*
Միսայէլ.	*ով խնդրուածք:*
Մնէս.	*լիար քանքար տես յեզէ. լբ.:*

	Mara,	bitter.
	Masałot',	the Book of Proverbs is said (thus).
	Masep't,	guardian.
295	Massa,	burden.
	Mat'ēos,	presented.
	Mart'a,	caller.
	Mariam,	elevated, or sea of bitterness.
	Melk'ia,	lord's king.
300	Melk'isedek,	king of justice.
	Melk'isua,	king saviour.
	Melk'oł.	who all.
	Memp'ibost'ē,	from shame's mouth.
	Mesołam,	peacemaker.
305	Mesopotania,	between river(s).
	Misp'at',	which is Kadēs, judgement.
	Mełk'a,	king.
	Mik'a,	poor.
	Mik'ayēl,	who is like god?
310	Misia,	ugly./
306v	Mik'ia,	who is like the lord?
	Misayēl,	who? question.
	Mnēs,	litre, talent, see Ezek. 38.

Մովաբ.   ի Հորէ:

315 Մովսա.   բարպրՕ կամ բենն:

Մովսէս.   ի ջրոյ Հանեալ:

Մոզ.   իմաստասէր կամ փիլո-

                  սոփոս:

Յակոբ.   խաբող:

Յամին.   աջ:

320 Յայէլ.   Համբարձումն կամ վայրի այծ:

Յայիէլ.   կենդանի է աստուած:

Յասն.   բժշկող:

Յաբէթ.   լայնացեալ:

Յերուս.   երուսաղէմ կամ աբացումն:

325 Յերապոլիս.   սուրբ քաղաք:

Յերուսթէ.   այր ամՕթոյ:

Յեմենի.   աջ:

Յէու.   ինքնինէն:

Յէուս.   խրատող կամ ցեց:

330 Յեսբոք.   է ունայն:

Յեսսէ.   էութիւն կամ էակ կամ

                  պարգեւ:

Յեսու.   տէր փրկիչ:

Յերորբադ.   մարանչող ընդ կոոց:

Յերորբվամ.   մարանչող ընդ ժողովրդեան:

Movab,	from father.
315 Movsa,	unleavened bread, or burden.
Movsēs,	drawn forth from water.
Mog,	lover of wisdom, or philoso-
	pher.
Yakob,	deceiver.
Yamin,	right hand.
320 Yayēl,	elevation, or goat of field.
Yayiēl,	god is living.
Yason,	healer.
Yabet',	having broadened.
Yebus,	Jerusalem, or kicking.
325 Yerapōlis,	sacred city.
Yebust'ē,	man of shame.
Yemeni,	right hand.
Yēu,	from self.
Yēus,	advisor, or moth.
330 Yespōk',	it is empty.
Yessē,	existence, or being, or
	offering.
Yesu,	lord, redeemer.
Yeroboał,	fighter with idol.
Yerobovam,	fighter with people.

335 Յեփթայէ.   բացող:

     Յիսուս.   տէր փրկիչ եբրայեցերէն

                      յեւսուայ:

     Յոթորայ.   վենագոյն: /

307ա Յեքոնիա.   պատրաստութիւն տեառն:

     Յոբ.   վշտագին կամ ողբացող:

340 Յուդայ.   գովութիւն:

     Յուլիոս.   բրատա:

     Յուննան.   աղաւնի:

     Յովաք.   հայրութիւն կամ ունող հայր:

     Յովակիմ.   տեառն յարութիւն:

345 Յովաս.   տեառն հուր կամ անմիաքան

                      կամ յուսահատեալ կամ ցեց:

     Յովաքիմ.   տեառն պատրաստութիւն:

     Յովէլ.   կամեցող կամ սկսանող:

     Յովհաննէս.   շնորհալի կամ արդար կամ

                      ողորմած:

     Յովնադաք.   կամաւոր:

350 Յովնա‹թ›ան.   տեառն պարգեւ:

     Յովնան.   արդար կամ ողորմած:

     Յովսափատ.   տէր դատաւոր:

     Յովսէփ.   տեառն աճումն:

     Յովսիա.   հուր տեառն:

335	Yep't'ayē,	opener.
	Yisus,	lord, saviour, in Hebrew
		Yēusuay
	Yot'ora,	supreme./
307r	Yek'onia,	lord's **pre**paration.
	Yob,	grievous, or lamenter.
340	Yuda,	praise.
	Yulios,	earthen (?).
	Yunan,	dove.
	Yovab,	paternity, or having a father.
	Yovakim,	lord's rising.
345	Yovas,	lord's fire, or disagreeing, or having despaired, or moth.
	Yovak'im,	lord's preparation.
	Yovēl,	desirer, or beginner.
	Yovhannēs,	gracious, or just, or merciful.
	Yovnadab,	willing.
350	Yovnat'an,	lord's offering.
	Yovnan,	just, or merciful.
	Yovsap'at.	lord judge.
	Yovsēp',	lord's increase.
	Yovsia,	lord's fire.

355 Յեղովմէ.　　　կարմիր կամ երկրային:

Յեգոնիա.　　　հազագանդութիւն տեառն:

Յովրամ.　　　բարձր կամ վեհագոյն:

Յորդանան.　　　զետ դատաստանի:

Յոքաս.　　　տեառն ըմբռնումն կամ ըմբռնող:

360 Յոյնք.　　　երրայեցերէն յելայիմ այս է

　　　　　　　խաբեբայք:

Նայասն.　　　oծ:

Նաբաթ.　　　կամաւոր:

Նաբադ.　　　աննիտ:

307բ Նաբովթ.　　　խորք/կամ մարգարէութիւն:

365 Նաբուգողոնոսոր.սուզ դատաստանի:

Նագարեթ.　　　սրբեալ կամ բաժանեալ կամ

　　　　　　　պահպանեալ կամ ծաղկեալ:

Նագովրացիք.　　　բաժանեալք կամ սրբաւլք:

Նաթան.　　　բաշխեալ կամ պարգեւեալ:

Նաթանայէլ.　　　պարգեւ աստուծոյ:

370 Նային.　　　գեղեցիկ:

Նաւում.　　　մխիթարիչ:

Նաբովր.　　　շորացեալ:

Նէեման.　　　գեղեցիկ:

Նէապոլիս.　　　նոր քաղաք:

355	Yedovmē,	red, or earthy.
	Yezonia,	lord's obedience.
	Yovram,	high or supreme.
	Yordanan,	river of judgement.
	Yok'az,	lord' seizing or seizer.
360	Yoynk',	in Hebrew Yewayim, that is deceivers.
	Nayason,	serpent.
	Nabat',	willing.
	Nabaɬ,	foolish.
307v	Nabovt',	pit,/or prophecy.
365	Nabugodonosor,	mourning of judgement.
	Nazaret',	sanctified, or separated, or guarded, or having flowered.
	Nazorac'ik',	separated ones, or sanctified ones.
	Nat'an,	distributed, or offered.
	Nat'anayēl,	god's offering.
370	Nayin,	beautiful.
	Naum,	comforter,
	Nak'ovr,	dried up.
	Nēeman,	beautiful.
	Nēapōlis,	new city.

375 Ներրովթ.   ապտամբ:

    Նէեմի.   մխիթարութիւն:

    Նէովստան.   պղնձի:

    Նեփթայիմ.   զուգաւորութիւն:

    Նինուէ.   գեղեցիկ:

380 Նոյ.   դադարումն կամ հանգիստ:

    Նոյոմին.   զարդարեալ կամ գեղեցիկ:

    Նուարեղղաբր.   գիրք թքւոց:

    Շաբաթ.   հանգիստ կամ դադարումն:

    Շուշանայ.   վարդ կամ շուշան:

385 Ոդողոմ.   վկայութիւն նոցա:

    Ոնէսիմէոս.   օգտակար:

    Ոզա.   զօրութիւն:

    Ոզիա.   զօրութիւն տեառն:

    Ոզիէլ.   զօրութիւն աստուծոյ: /

308ա 390 Ողա.   վրաս կամ խորան:

    Ոննամ.   վիշտ:

    Ովբաթիայ.   ծառայ տեառն:

    Ովբէթ.   ծառայ:

    Ովբ.   քաղարծ:

395 Ովնանայ.   վիշտ կամ անիրաւութիւն

    Ովսէէ.   փրկիչ:

    Ովրէփ.   ագռաւ:

    Որդի եկրայ.   գիրք դեւտական:

375	Nebrovt',	rebellion.
	Nēemi,	consolation.
	Nēovstan,	of bronze.
	Nep't'ayim,	equality.
	Ninuē,	beautiful.
380	Noy,	cessation, or rest.
	Noyomin,	decorated, or beautiful.
	Nuareddabr,	Book of Numbers.
	Šabat',	rest, or cessation.
	Šušanay,	rose, or lily.
385	Odoɫom,	their witness.
	Onēsimēos,	helpful.
	Oza,	might.
	Ozia,	lord's might.
	Oziēl,	god's might. /
308r 390	Oɫa,	tent, or pavilion.
	Ornam,	affliction.
	Ovbat'ia,	lord's servant.
	Ovbēt',	servant.
	Ovk',	unleavened bread.
395	Ovnanay,	suffering, or injustice.
	Ovsēē,	saviour.
	Ovrēp',	raven.
	Ordi ekra,	Book of Leviticus.

	Ուրիայ.	հուր տեառն:
400	Որգիայ.	ընքրունումն:
	Պաղիստինէ.	մոխրով արկեալ:
	Պարասկեւէ.	պատրաստութիւն:
	Պասեք.	անցք:
	Պենտէկոստ.	յիսներորդ:
405	Պետրոս.	վէմ:
	Զերոնիմոս.	սուրբ անուն:
	Ռաբաթ.	յոլով կամ մեծ:
	Ռագուէլ.	հովիւ աստուծոյ:
410	Ռահաբ.	ամբարտաւան կամ քաշ:
	Ռախաբ.	լայնացեալ:
	Ռամայ.	վերամբարձ:
	Ռամեսէ.	որոտումն գեգոյ:
	Ռափայէլ.	բժշկութիւն կամ դեղ աստուծոյ:
	Ռափայիմ.	հսկայք կամ բժիշկք:
415	Ռաքէլ.	ոչխար:
	Ռեմոն.	նոնենի: /
308ք	Ռնսփայ.	սատկութիւն:
	Ռեբեկայ.	կուշտ:
	Ռեքաբ.	կառք:
420	Ռուբէն.	տեսանող գործի:
	Ռորովամ.	բազմացուցանող գժողովուրդ:
	Սաբայ.	դարձումն կամ գերութիւն կամ շրջագայութիւն:
	Սաբաովթ.	գօրք:

	Uria,	lord's fire.
400	Ok'oziƨ,	seizure.
	Paɬistinē,	cast of ashes.
	Paraskewē,	preparation.
	Pasek',	passing.
	Pentēkost,	fiftieth.
405	Petros,	rock.
	J̆eronimos,	holy name.
	Ṙabat',	great, or large.
	Ṙaguēl,	god's shepherd.
410	Ṙahab,	proud, or brave.
	Ṙaxab,	broadened.
	Ṙama,	elevated.
	Ṙamesē,	thunder of moth.
	Ṙap'ayēl,	healing or medicine of god.
	Ṙap'ayim	giants or doctors.
415	Ṙak'ēl,	sheep.
	Ṙemon,	pomegranate-tree./
	Ṙesp'a,	violence.
	Ṙebeka,	side.
	Ṙek'ab,	chariot.
420	Ṙ ubēn,	seeing the son.
	Robovam,	increasing the people.
	Saba,	return, or captivity, or going around.
	Sabaovt',	armies.

308v

	Սադուկեցիք	արդարք :
425	Սադա.	առաքումն :
	Սադիմ.	խաղաղութիւն :
	Սադմանասար.	խաղաղութիւն հաստատեալ :
	Սադմոն.	խաղաղարար :
	Սադպադ.	Յովանի երկիւղի :
430	Սամարիա.	պահապանութիւն :
	Սամփսոն.	արեգական նորա կամ անուան
		կրկնութիւն :
	Սամուէլ.	ընդել յաստուծոյ :
	Սառայ.	տիրուհի կամ անեւշահոտ :
	Սատանայ.	ոսոխ կամ փոխ առեալ :
435	Սարայի.	տիրուհի իմ :
	Սարոնայ.	մակրդակ :
	Սաուղ.	խնդրեալ կամ արուեստ :
	Սափատ.	դատող :
	Սեդէկիա.	արդար տեառն :
440	Սեդիմ.	տարածումն :
	Սէթ.	եղեալ :
	Սեգովւր.	փոքր :
	Սելում.	խաղաղարար կամ մնացող :
	Սեհոն.	արմատախիլ : /
309ա 445	Սեդովմ.	յատակող :
	Սեմ.	անուն կամ համբաւ կամ եղեալ :

		Sadukec'ik',	just ones.
	425	Saƚa,	sending.
		Saƚim,	peace.
		Saƚmanasar,	established peace.
		Saƚmon,	peace-maker.
		Saƚpaad,	shadow of fear.
	430	Samaria,	guarding.
		Samp'son,	his sun, or repetition of name.
		Samuēl,	accustomed by god.
		Sara,	mistress, or sweet-smelling.
		Satana,	adversary, or having borrowed.
	435	Sarayi,	my mistress.
		Sarona,	⌈ one word ⌉
		Sawuƚ,	having asked, or fox.
		Sap at,	judge.
		Sedēkia,	lord's just one.
	440	Sedim,	extension.
		Sēt',	placed.
		Segor,	small.
		Selum,	peace-maker, or remaining.
		Sehon,	rooted out./
309r	445	Seƚovm,	destroyer.
		Sem,	name, or fame, or placed.

Սեմէի․	հնազանդ կամ ա՛նուն իմ։
Սենեքերիմ․	մօրենի աւերման։
Սէոն․	հնչումն։
450 Սեփովրայ․	գեղեցիկ կամ փող կամ թռչուն կամ ձրնձղուկ։
Սելովամ․	առաքեալ կամ առաքող։
Սիբայ․	գործ։
Սիբողդէթ․	բենն։
Սիմէովն․	լսող կամ լուր։
455 Սիմոն․	հնազանդ։
Սին․	մօրենի կամ զէն կամ վահան։
Սիոն․	կոյտ։
Սիսարայ․	գծիծառն տեսանող։
Սիւքեմ․	բազուկ։
460 Սէքոր․	սեաւ կամ խառնեալ կամ նեղոս։
Սկարիովտացի․	այր սպանութեան։
Սոդոմ․	խորհուրդ նոցա։
Սոմեր․	պահապան։
Սովմացի․	ննջող։
465 Սորեկ․	այգի։
Սոփիդիմ․	դատաւորք․
Ստեփաննոս․	պսակեալ։
Վաքարովդ․	ուր փառք կամ վայ փառաց։
Տարսոս․	թեւաւոր։

Semei,	obedient, or my name.
Senēk'ērim,	thorn-bush of destruction.
Sēon,	noise.
450 Sep'ovra,	beautiful, or trumpet, or bird, or sparrow.
Selovam,	sent, or sender.
Siba,	army.
Sibołet',	burden.
Simēon,	hearer, or hearing.
455 Simōn,	obedient.
Sin,	thorn-bush, or weapon, or shield.
Sion,	heap.
Sisara,	seeing the sparrow.
Siwk'em,	arm.
460 Sik'or	black, or mixed, or Nile.
Skariovtac'i,	man of killing.
Sodom,	their secret.
Somēr,	guard.
Sovmnac'i,	sleeper.
465 Sorek,	vineyard.
Sop'idim,	judges.
Step'annos,	crowned.
Vak'abovd,	where glory, or woe of glory.
Tarsos,	winged.

470 Տիմէոս.　　　　կոյր կամ կուրութիւն:

Տիմոթէոս.　　　　պատիւ աստուծոյ յունաց է
　　　　　　　　　բառ:/

309բ　Տիտոս.　　　　պատուական:

Տիւրացիք.　　　　նեղացեալք:

Տուբիայ.　　　　բարի տէր:

475 Փակէէ.　　　　բացող:

Փանուէլ.　　　　տեսանող զաստուած:

Փասկա.　　　　բլուր:

Փարաւոն.　　　　գրուող:

Փարէզ.　　　　բաժանումն կամ ձիաւոր:

480 Փարիսեցիք.　　　　բաժանեալք:

Փենէ՛էզ.　　　　երես հաւատոյ:

Փոքոր.　　　　վիհ:

Փութ.　　　　ափրիկայ:

Փաղեկ.　　　　բաժանումն:

485 Քաղդեաստան.　　　　եբրայեցերէն կազդին այս է իբրեւ
　　　　　　　　　դեւք:

Քազբի.　　　　ստախօսք:

Քաղէք.　　　　իբրեւ զսիրտ:

Քամ.　　　　ջերմ կամ ջերմութիւն:

Քանան.　　　　վաճառական:

490 Քեբրոն.　　　　բարեկամութիւն կամ ընկերութիւն:

Քետուրա.　　　　անուշահոտ:

470 Timēos,   blind, or blindness.

    Timot'ēos,   god's honour, it is a Greek
                    word./

309v   Titos,   honourable.

        Tiwrac'ik',   afflicted ones.

        Tubiay,   good lord.

475 P'akēē,   opener.
    P'anuēl,   seeing God.

        P'aska,   hill.

        P'arawou,   scatterer.

        P'arez,   division, or equestrian.

480 P'arisec'ik, divided ones.

        P'enēnēz,   face of faith.

        P'ok'or,   gulf.

        P'ut',   Africa.

        P'aɫek,   division.

485 K'aɫdeastan, Hebrew Kazdin, that is: like
                    demons.

        K'azbi,   speaker of lies.

        K'aɫeb,   like the heart.

        K'am,   hot or heat.

        K'anan,   merchant.

490 K'ebron,   friendship or company.

        K'etura,   sweet-smelling.

Քор．　　　　　լեառն：

Քորեբ．　　　անապատ：

Քորազին．　　խորհուրդ：

495　Քուշ．　　　եթովբացի：

Քուս．　　　　խրատ：

Քրիստոս．　　օծեալ：

K'or,   mountain.

K'oreb,   desert.

K'orazin,   secret.

495   K'uš,   Ethiopian.

K'us,   counsel.

K'ristos,   anointed.

1　 յեքրայեցոց 55 81 　　　2 ՝այր} 88 　om 55 　|
3　 անցանօրք 55 　　　4 ապտիւ 55 　　　8 ապեթնագով 55
10　 յունայնութիւն 55 　　　11 ապքենէք 55 　　　14 ապի-
այթար 55 　　　16 ապիմէլէք} 55 　արդիմելէք 81
17　 ապինաթար 55 　　　19 om 55 　　　21 ապրամմ } 55
ապրամմ 81 　　　23 ագաք} 55 　ագա՝ 81 　　　26 պանտուխդ
55 　　　27 յերկնային 55 　| 　կարմի 81 　　　28 ադոնայ
55 　　　29 ադոնայի} 55 ·ադոնիա 81 　　　30 ադոնիայ·
տիրոդ 55 　　31 ագարիայ 55 　　　32 կոդուպուտ 55
34　 աթադիայ 55 　　　38 ալելուիա 81 　| օր՝նեցէք 55
39　 ալեքսանդեր 81 　| 　քաչ 55 　　　40 ադեքսանդրիա 55|
եքրա 55 81 　| 　նոյ} 81 　om 55 　| 　՝ուս} 55 ՝րոոմ
81 　　41 ամադէկ 55 　　　44 ամանա 55 　　　46 տէրու-
թիւն 55 　　　47 ամեսայի քաչ 55 　　　48 ամեսայի} 55
ամէսիա 81 　　　49 ՝աստատ 55 　　　51 ամոն 55
53　 քաչ ՝այրն եսայեա + մարգարէին erased 55 　| 　է } 81
om 　55 　　　54 մարգարէն է} 55 　om 81 　　　56 աննանիայ
55 　　　58 ուրախար 55 　　　61 անտիոքայ 55 　　　62
ապոդոս 55 　　　68 ասքայ 55 　　　74 արիքակոս 55
արիսապոս 88 　　　76 արտաքսերքէս 55 　արտաքսերսէս 81
| 　՝ատայզգայթ 55 　| 　անէծ 81 　　　77 արքագամթ 81
78　 եդքայր 55 　| 　՝օր} 55 　տեատն 81 　　　79 ապիմելէք
55 　80 ապայիայ 55 　　　82 ապիտորէլ 55 　ակիտոփէլ 81
84　 քաթուէ որդիութիւն 55 　　　86 after ln 88 55 　|
ոաքէլայ 55 　| 　ծեռացեալ կամ զարՙուրեալ } 55 om 81
87　 totum om 　81 　　　89 քալլայ 55 　　　91 քաներգէս
55 　　92 քատո 55 　　　94 քարիովնայ 55 　　　98 քար-
տէմէոս 55 　　　99 քէեդ զեքիւդ 55 　　　101 քեթանիայ
55 　　　103 քեդթաւան 81 　　　104 քէթէլ 55 　　　105
քէթէր 55 　　　106 քեդդա՝էմ 81 　　　107 դուսար} տուն
55 　　　108 քեդսաքէէ 81 　　　109 քեդսամիուս 81
110　 քեդսայիդայ 81 　　　111 քեդքագէ 81 　　　112 քեդ-
քագովր 81 　| 　անդրնդոց 55 　　　114 քելքեգովր 81
115　 քէ՝սմովթ 81 　　　121 քեթագոն 55 　| 　ցորենոյ 55
123　 քէլայ 55 　　　126 քէրէսիթ 55 　　　127 գապայա 55
128　 գաքայաթ 55 　　　131 գաթգաթ 55 　　　գոքեդ } գոքք

55   137 գէթոն 55   143 գլուխ 81[*] գլուխք 81°
| դնի 81   144 գողիաղ 81   145 գոլմոր 55
146 գոմորա 55   149 դալիա 55   150 դաղան 55
151 բոցո 81   153 աստուծոյ } om 55   158 դիա-
պոլոս 81   159 դիդիմնոս 55   162 դէոնէսիոս 81
166 ՝նունեան} 55 ՝նազանդունեան 81   170 եգլով
55   173 եգէկիայ 55   174 եգէկիէլ 55   178
բաչունիւն 55   179 եթովփիայ 55 | յունարէն} 81
om 55   սէվունիւն 55   180 ելզանա 55   181
ելեքանան 55   182 եղիայ 55   185 եղիմէլեք 55 |
իմ } 81   om 55   189 եկլեսիաստէս 55 եկլիսիաստէկես
81   192 նաւակատիք 55   196 եսայիա 55   199
om 81   200 երամմէլ 55   204 կենդա 55   205
երրաթայ 55 եփրայ 81   206 երրայիմ 55   208
զաքոն 55   210 զարա 55   213 զեքեթեա 55
215 ամոթոյ 55   216 զլլեսմովդ 55   217 Թաթէոս
55   219 թարա 55   222 թաքոր 81   224
< Թոքէլ >} Թոփէլ 55 Թոքէլ 81   225 Թով 55
230 իսքար 55   232 իէլ . 81   233 լիայ 55
235 լիքիայ 55   236 քարամք շարեալ 55   238
խաթէս 55   243 կարիթարիմ 55   244 կարիաթսնվէր
55   251 կեփաս} illeg sign tollows   55   252
կինովդ 55   254 կելէոպաս 55   259 կամ 2° } om
55   ՝այեասաան 81   262 բնծա 55   263 ՝ելի-
պոլիս 55   266 բաչ 55 | գորեդ 55[*]   271
լամեք 55 | խոնար՝ել 55   273 դեղեւի 55   275
դեք 55   279 մայաբեա 55   285 մաղադեթ 55
287 ծնեալ 55   293 մաաաղովթ 55   294 մասեփայ
55   297 մարթա 55   299 մելքիայ 55 | տէր 55
300 մելքիսեթեկ 55   304 մնսապոտանիայ 55   307
om 55   308 om 81   314 մովափ 55   315
մովաս 81   317 փիլոսփայ 55[*]   320 ՝ամբարձեալ
55 327 յէմէնի 55   329 յենւ 55   333 մարանոդ
81   335 յեքթայէ 55   339 ողբացոդ} 55 աղբեցոդ
81   341 բրդոտ 55   343 յովափ 55   349-351
om 81   350 յովնաթան } յովնադան 55

352 յովսափթ 55   354 յովսիայ 55   355 յեթովմէ
55   357 վեՇպգոյն 55   359 յոբագ 55   365
նանբոգոթոնոսոր 55   368 նանթան 55 | բաշխեալ
81   պարգեւել 55   369 աստուծոյ }   + նային պարգեւ
աստուծոյ 55   373 նէման 55   375 նեբրովդ 55
376 նէմի 55   377 նէոստան պղրնծի 55   378
նեփայիմ 55   382 Նուարեդդաբեր գիրգ 55   383
նաբաթ 55   384 շուշաննայ 55   387 nqա } 55
ուլա 81   qopnւթիւն---qopnւթիւն (ln 888)} om   55:
hmt   392 ողբաղիայ 81   395 ովնաննա 55   397
ովէփ ռազաւ 81   398 դեւտական գիրք 55   399
ուրիա 55   400 օբոգիա 55   401 պաղեսղինէ 55 |
մովբով 81   404 պեննակոստ 55   406 ջերոՆիմոս
55   408 Ꜧովիվ 55   410 բաշ 55   413
ռպփայէլ 55   414 ռայփայիմ բմիշք 55   416 ռեմմոն 55
417 ռեփա 55   418 ռեբեկա 55   419 om 81
420 ռոբէն 55   421 գզողովուրոն 55   422 սառա
55   423 սափավովթ 55   425 81   426
սաղէմ 55   429 սաղապաթ 55   430 սամբսոն 81 |
արեզակ 81 | կրթուθիւն 81   432 ընդել} 81 եղեաւ
55   433 սառա 55   434 սատանա 55   435
սարոնա 55   436 աղուէստ 55   438 սափթ 55
441 սէդ 81   442 սեզորով 55   443 սելլում 55
444 սեꜧեն արմատաꜧիլ 81   447 սիմէի 55   448
սեննրիմ 55   449 սեոն 55   450 սեփովրա 55
452 սիբա 55   453 սիբոդեդ 81 457 սիննոյն 55
458 սիսարա գծիծռան 55   461 սպաննուθեան 55
463 սեմեր 81   464 սոմնացի 55   465 յայզի 55
468 վայբայբովդ 55   470 կոռուθիւն 55   477
փասբայ 81   478 ցրւօղ 81   479 փարէս 55
480 փարեսեցիք 55   484 փաղեք 55   485 բաղ-
դէասսան 55   կասθին 55   486 ստաիսօղ 81   487
բաղէփ 55   490 բեփրոն 55   բարեկամուθիւն} 81
բարեբաննւθիւն 55   493 բորէփ 55

ln 2   Ona III ln 2.

ln 3   Ona III ln 1.

ln 4   Contrast Ona III ln 5, Ona I ln 6A, "Abdiu,
        promised servant". Compare the text of Wutz'
        Greek group V 1 Ἀβδίοῦ, δουλεύων κυρίῳ
        (p. 705), Coisl, 10 (p. 714), Ona II ln 5
        Աբդիու. ծառայելով : "Abdiu, by serving".

ln 5   Ona III ln 4.

ln 6   Ona III ln 6.

ln 7   Not in Ona II, III. Is comparable, but not
        identical with Ona I ln 57, cf. variae lectio-
        nes there.

ln 8   Ona III ln 3.

ln 9   Abel appears as "mourning" in Ona I, II. No
        exact parallel to the text here appears in any
        of Wutz' lists.

ln 10   Ona III ln 8.

ln 11   Compare Ona I, ln 51 "father or son of candle".

ln 12   Ona III ln 18.

ln 13   Ona III ln 10.

ln 14   Ona III ln 11 is similar but not identical: cf.
        Ona I ln 43.

ln 15   This etymology for "Abigayil", Ona III ln 14.
        See Wutz p. 483 on variation of form.

ln 16   Ona III ln 16. The reading of 81 "Abdimelēk"
        is corrupt.

ln 17   Cf. Ona III ln 19. Wutz (p. 100**2**) points out
that the etymologies of "Nadab" names in Ona III
show an original <u>sponsalis</u> instead of the correct <u>spontalis</u> or <u>spontanaeus</u>, suggesting an
origin of at least some of the etymologies of
Ona III in a Latin onomasticon. Note, however,
that this present list reads "willing". It also
differs in its translation from Ona I ln 15.

ln 18   No parallels to this name and etymology are
evident in Wutz' materials.

ln 19   Ona III ln 17:55 omits completely.

ln 20   Ona III ln 21.

ln 21   Ona III ln 23: the form "Abra(h)am" is correct,
cf. MS 55. The confusion of "Abraham" and
"Abram" is common in the onomastica.

ln 22   Ona III ln 22.

ln 23   Compare Ona III, ln 24: the form of the name
there is <u>Agabos</u>, which also occurs at Ona I with
a different etymology. "Locust" occurs only
here and in Ona III, deriving from Hebrew
חגב; cf. Wutz, p. 963, n. 24.

ln 24   The etymology for "Agag" in Ona III ln 25 uses
a different word for "roof" and is combined with
that for "Agal". See also Wutz, pp. 483f.

ln 25   Ona III, ln 37.

ln 26   Ona III, ln 26, Ona II ln 56.

ln 27   In Ona III ln 28 the wording is different. Wutz
has *երկաւոր* "twin" for *երկրաւոր* "earthly", presumably printer's error. In MS 55 *յերկկաւոր*
"heavenly" is found, a not uncommon confussion,
see Arm IV Ezra 6:20 D.

ln 28   Ona III ln 29.

ln 29   Ona III ln 30: the form found in MS 55 is pre-
           ferable to the "Adona" of MS 81, see next ln.
           Wutz, note ad loc sees a mistranslation from
           Latin in Ona III which read domini mei as a
           genitive singular instead of a nominative plu-
           ral. The plural is presented here.

ln 30   Ona III ln 31.

ln 31   Ona III ln 32.

ln 32   Ona III ln 34, Ona II ln 17.

ln 33   "Azotos", i.e. Ashdod; Ona II, ln 17, Ona III,
           ln 33.

ln 34   Ona III ln 35.

ln 35   Ona III ln 38.

ln 36   Ona III ln 39.

ln 37   Ona III ln 40.

ln 38   Cf. Ona III ln 41, Ona I ln 56. The forms in
           MS 55 for lns 38 9 with ⁊ "ł" have been pre-
           ferred, as the alphabetical order requires.
           These are also the more ancient. In ln 40,
           too, MS 55 has been followed for consistency's
           sake.

ln 39   See Ona III ln 42 and Wutz, note in loc.

ln 40   Ona III ln 43. ꞇnⱡⱀ "cruel" or "raw" is the
           reading there as in MS 55. In MS 81 there is
           a corrupt reading ꞇⱀnnⱀ "Rome".

ln 41   Unlike Ona III ln 44, Ona I ln 29. Equivalent
           to Ona III ln 51, "Amełik, king".

ln 42   Ona III ln 45.

ln 43   Ona III ln 47 for similar etymology but differ-
           ent wording.

ln 44   Ona III ln 46.

ln 45   i.e. Habakkuk; no parallel to this etymology is
           to be found among Wutz' texts.

ln 46   Cf. Ona III lns 60-61. This entry disturbs the
           alphabetical order.

ln 47   Cf. Ona III ln 48; but there the wording dif-
           fers. The name there is "Amasayi", cf. ln 55
           "Amesayi", here. See ln 48.

ln 48   Cf. Ona III ln 49: but there the wording dif-
           fers. The form of name in MS 55 has been pre-
           ferred to "Amesia" of MS 81. It resembles Ona
           III ln 49, fits the alphabetical order, and
           provides a basis for the etymology עַם + שִׁי .

ln 49   Ona III ln 52.

ln 50   Cf. Ona III ln 53 and commentary on ln 17, supra.

ln 51   Ona III ln 54.

ln 52   Ona III ln 55: but there "Amnon".

ln 53   Cf. Ona III ln 57.

ln 54   Cf. Ona III ln 58: the words "it is the pro-
           phet" found only in MS 55, seem on the basis of
           Ona III to be original.

ln 55   i.e. "the Amorite"; Ona III ln 56.

ln 56   Ona III, ln 62.

ln 57   Cf. Ona I ln 33: there the words "or song" are
           not found.

ln 58   Cf. Ona I ln 80 "Angē, feasts" which is found
         in Greek (Wutz, pp. 694, 740) and Syriac
         (Wutz, pp. 793, 829, et.al.).

ln 59   Cf. Ona III ln 63: different wording.

ln 60   This exact interpretation does not occur else-
         where. For another based on χάρις etc. see
         Ona III ln 64 and for discussion of the stem in
         Onomastica, see Wutz, pp. 106 ff.

ln 61   Ona III ln 65: wording differs.

ln 62   No Armenian parallels. For the type of reading
         serving as a source for this, see Wutz, p. 457,
         deriving from stem   פלי״א and perhaps, by trans-
         position, אלי״פ . A Greek Ἀπολλῶς also exists,
         ibid.

ln 63   Cf. Ona III ln 69.

ln 64   See Esther 1:9 etc., Greek ἀστιν. No parallels
         exist in Wutz' lists.

ln 65   Ona III ln 71 : there is no parallel to վերա-
         ւոη"ascender, one who ascends".

ln 66   Ona III ln 70.

ln 67   Ona III ln 72: wording differs.

ln 68   Cf. Ona III ln 93: the name there is "Ak'sa".

ln 69   i.e. Arabians; see Ona III 94: the word երե-
         կւան generally means "belonging to yesterday".
         This must be an inner-Armenian confusion for
         "of the evening", as is indicated by Ona III
         ibid.

ln 70   i.e. Arabians, Ona III ln 75: wording differs.

ln 71   Ona III ln 76.

ln 72   Ona III lns 77-78

ln 73   See Ona I, variant reading, Wutz p. 866 n., cf.
           Ona III ln 79.

ln 74   Ona III ln 82: the text of 81 contains a gra-
           phic corruption *n* <u>o</u> > *u* <u>s</u>, producing the reading
           "Arispagos". The correction is supported by
           Ona III <u>ibid</u>.

ln 75   Ona I, Wutz p. 852 n. to ln 22.

ln 76   Ona III ln 86: the text is restored on the
           basis of the readings of MSS 55 and 81.

ln 77   Ona III ln 87.

ln 78   Ona III ln 88: MS 81 reads եղբայր տեառն
           "lord's brother" which appears corrupt.

ln 79   Ona III ln 91: MS 55 reads Աբիմելէք "Abimelēk"
           which appears corrupt.

ln 80   Cf. Ona III ln 89: the wording differs.

ln 81   Ona III ln 90.

ln 82   Ona III ln 92.

ln 83   Cf. Ona III ln 97: "shame" arises from a dif-
           ferent interpretation of the idea of confusion.

ln 84   Ona I ln 132 reads, as would be expected,
           "daughter of God". MS 55 "Bat'uē, sonship of
           God" is no more explicable than the text of MS
           81 is given here.

ln 85   Ona III ln 94: difference in wording.

ln 86 Cf. Ona I ln 133 and Wutz, pp. 281-2 for mean-
     ing "aged". No parallel for "amazed" (an ety-
     mology doubtless derived from Hebrew בהל) seems
     to occur in Wutz. MS 55 is somewhat fuller than
     MS 81 at this point and has some variation in
     the order of names; see apparatus. This and
     the following names commencing with "B" are not
     included in Ona III.

ln 87 No parallels to this etymology of the name oc-
     cur in Wutz' materials. For its basis, see the
     preceding note.

ln 88 The etymology remains without clear parallel.

ln 89 The etymology is almost quite without parallel.
     For "swallower", however, see Wutz, p. 251 and
     material assembled there. The original spell-
     ing was doubtless with η "ı".

ln 90 Unparalleled etymology, based on בן + יה . A
     different etymology for the name is Ona I ln
     157.

ln 91 Ona I ln 172.

ln 92 No parallel in the lists. Compare Wutz, p. 327.
     A transcription of the Hebrew measurement בת .

ln 93 Ona I ln 149.

ln 94 Ona I ln 170.

ln 95 The name and etymology do not occur in Ona I.
     They are found in Greek, see the list printed
     by Wutz, p. 681.

ln 96 Ona I ln 177.

ln 97 Ona I ln 166: slight difference in wording.

ln 98   The name and etymology do not occur in Ona I.
           They are found in Greek, see the list printed
           by Wutz, p. 709.

ln 99   Ona I ln 176: wording differs.

ln 100   The etymology does not occur elsewhere. For
           "ray", cf. "Barak" above. For "difficult,
           hard" no parallel is found.

ln 101   Cf. Ona I ln 174 variae lectiones with a dif-
           ference of wording. See very close Greek par-
           allel, Wutz, p. 713.

ln 102   The name and etymology do not occur in Ona I or
           elsewhere in the lists. No clear basis for "of
           passings" can be found.

ln 103   No parallels exist in the Armenian or Greek
           lists. Compare the Latin, Wutz, p. 147.

ln 104   Ona I ln 150.

ln 105   No parallel in Wutz. Apparently etymology
           derives from בתי"ר.

ln 106   Ona I ln. 156.

ln 107   The reading "daughter" may be found in Ona I ln
           139. It is no less strange than the reading
           "house" of MS 55, which is a dittography of the
           following. This etymology belongs, presumably
           to "Bathsheba" and not to "Beersheba", although
           a different etymology is given for that name by
           Ona I ln. 152. The confusion is ancient, cf.
           Wutz, p. 691. Here, however, the alphabetical
           order indicates that it is independent of the
           Greek confusion and arose in Armenian.

ln 108   For this etymology, see Wutz, p. 775. The
          etymology of this name in Ona I varies.

ln 109   Ona I ln 154.

ln 110   The etymologies for this name are derived
          from בית זית or בית ציד . Ona I ln 173 reads
          Ἐλεου for Ἐλαιας. The origins of the pres-
          ent reading therefore remain obscure.

ln 111   In Wutz, p. 707 "house of mouth or pharynx"
          is found in Greek and slightly different
          readings occur elsewhere (see Wutz, Index,
          s.v.). The reading here derives from this by
          a corruption of φάρυγξ to φάραγξ "gully,
          ravine". Ona I ln 175 is based on a differ-
          ent Greek tradition.

ln 112   For the name, see the Latin quoted by Wutz,
          p. 475. No parallel to the etymology given
          here was found.

ln 113   No clear parallels to the etymology "treach-
          erous" were found. For "without yoke", com-
          pare the Latin list given by Wutz, p. 772
          absque iugo.

ln 114   i.e. Baal Peor; the etymology does not
          accord with that given in the other Onomasti-
          ca. It is based on the same interpretation
          as line 112, deriving from בעל and פער .

ln 115   The name and etymology have no parallel in
          the lists, but their origin is transparent.

ln 116   Ona I ln 134.

ln 117   Not in Ona I, but in Cyril of Alexandria,
          Wutz, p. 1059 and Latin, Wutz, p. 579.

ln 118   Not in Ona I or Greek. For Latin parallel,
          see Wutz, p. 118, n. 1.

ln 119   Cf. Ona I ln 144.

ln 120   The name occurs with a different etymology in
          Ona I, ln 139. For this etymology, see Syri-
          ac list (Wutz, p. 793) and Theodoret (Wutz,
          p. 1061).

ln 121   Cf. Wutz, p. 649.

ln 122   Wutz, p. 346.

ln 123   See ln 89 for the etymology. The name is un-
          known in this form.

ln 124   Ona III ln 98.

ln 125   Ona I ln 167.

ln 126   The name also occurs in Ona I, but with a
          different etymology.

ln 127   Ona III ln 99.

ln 128   The name occurs elsewhere, e.g. Ona III ln
          101, but the etymology remains without paral-
          lel.

ln 129   Ona III ln 103.

ln 130   "Gat̄" 55:   cf. Ona III ln 105 with different
          wording. With "arriving quickly", compare
          Wutz, pp. 689, 720.

ln 131   Cf. Ona III ln 104: wording differs.

ln 132   No parallels to the etymology are evident. It
          derives from a common meaning of ד"מ ג.

ln 133   Ona III ln 113: wording differs.

ln 134   i.e. "Galatians"; no parallels to the ety-
          mology are evident.

ln 135   Cf. Ona III ln 112.

ln 136   Cf. Ona III ln 115: wording is different.

ln 137   Cf. Ona III ln 116: wording is quite differ-
          ent.

ln 138   Or "breast": Ona III ln 123.

ln 139   Ona III ln 117: some difference of wording.

ln 140   Ona I ln 209: Ona III ln 120 varies.

ln 141   No etymology is given for the name by either
          MS 55 or MS 81.

ln 142   Ona III ln 127 has the same etymology but a
          different word. Compare ln 24 supra.

ln 143   Ona III ln 129.

ln 144   Compare Ona III ln 124: see also Wutz, pp.
          169 f.

ln 145   This is apparently a variant for "Gomer", cf.
          Ona III ln 130, Ona I ln 207.

ln 146   Cf. Ona III ln 131, with a variant of the
          name.

ln 147   Ona I ln 264 apparatus criticus.

ln 148   Ona III ln 133: different wording.

ln 149   Ona III ln 135.

ln 150   Ona III ln 134: different wording.

ln 151   Ona III lns 136-137.

ln 152   Ona III ln 138.

ln 153   Ona III ln 139.

ln 154   Ona III ln 140: wording differs.

ln 155   Ona III ln 142: wording differs somewhat.

ln 156   Ona III ln 143.

ln 157   Ona III ln 144: the genitive case is under-
           standable in Ona III but not in the present
           list.

ln 158   This etymology occurs in both Greek and Latin
           sources, see Wutz, p. 650.

ln 159   The etymology lacks in both manuscripts.

ln 160   Ona III ln 150.

ln 161   Not in Ona III; cf. in general Ona I, ln 247
           and apparatus criticus there, Wutz, p. 618.
           The meaning "judger (or: judging)" is unparal-
           leled.

ln 162   Ona III ln 149. The spelling of MS 55 is
           clearly required by the alphabetical order.

ln 163   Ona III ln 154: different wording.

ln 164   "Generation" in the sense of "origin", cf. Ona
           III ln 152.

ln 165   Ona III ln 153.

ln 166   See Ona III ln 198: Compare Wutz' important
           comments, p. 381. The parallels support the
           reading "of antiquity"of MS 55 rather than
           Հնազանդութեան "of obedience" of MS 81. This
           is probably an inner-Armenian development.

ln 167   Ona III lns 325-326.

ln 168   i.e. "Hebrew"; Ona III ln 322: the ʰ "h" in Ona III lns 322, 325-6 suggests a non-Greek origin there.

ln 169   The word ὑϐηηιωδρ "afflictions" is rare. The name and etymology do not appear in II and III. Compare, however, Ona I ln 282.

ln 170   Ona III ln 200.

ln 171   Ona III ln 201.

ln 172   Ona III ln 202 "red" (different word); cf. ln 27 above.

ln 173   Ona III ln 203.

ln 174   In Ona III ln 204 we read "god's help", cf. Ona II ln 27. The reading here accords with ln 172 and with the examples on Wutz, p. 807 ln 24, p. 829 ln 112, p. 1001 ln 23, et al.

ln 175   Cf. Ona III ln 242: difference in wording.

ln 176   Ona III ln 204.

ln 177   The name is perhaps parallel to that found in the Latin material quoted by Wutz, p. 781, but if so, then the etymologies are quite different. From the etymology, one might assume that the form of the name was "Ezron" רון + חן . If so, compare Ona I ln 275, and חצרון (Wutz, Index, s.v.). The etymology here is unknown although some analogous forms exist.

ln 178   Cf. Ona III ln 206: difference in wording.

ln 179   With the latter part of the etymology, cf. Origen quoted by Wutz, p. 740. No clear parallels to the first part occur in Wutz.

ln 180   This etymology, based on אל + קנא is quite
          different from that found in the Greek sources
          listed by Wutz or in Ona I ln 302. No paral-
          lels are to be found.

ln 181   See Ona I ln 302, 444; Wutz, p. 515. "Mercy"
          is unusual.

ln 182   Ona III ln 214.

ln 183   Ona III ln 213.

ln 184   Ona III ln 213.

ln 185   Ona III ln 217: difference in wording.

ln 186   This name does not appear in any of the sources
          adduced by Wutz nor in the Bible or New Testa-
          ment. The etymology is obvious.

ln 187   Ona III ln 224. Note there the non-Armenian
          form of the name.

ln 188   Ona III ln 215.

ln 189   Ona III ln 207: difference in wording. The
          reading "Eklisiastikēs" is apparently inner-
          Armenian.

ln 190   Ona III ln 235.

ln 191   Ona III ln 237.

ln 192   There appear to be no parallels to the name or
          etymology.

ln 193   Ona III ln 239.

ln 194   Ona III ln 165.

ln 195   The etymology appears to be without any paral-
          lel. Contrast Ona III ln 166.

ln 196   Ona III ln 168.

ln 197   Ona III   ln 241.

ln 198   Ona III   ln 170:   slight difference in word-
            ing.

ln 199   This name is omitted by MS 81 and is out of
            alphabetical order in MS 55.   It does not
            occur in the other Armenian onomastica, but
            the name is found in Latin quoted by Wutz,
            p. 482.   The etymology is quite obvious.

ln 200   Ona III   ln 422:   "lord's mercy".   The read-
            ing "god's"   seems more accurate.

ln 201   Ona III   ln 424.

ln 202   Ona III   ln 425:   difference in wording.

ln 203   Ona III   ln 256.

ln 204   Cf. Ona I ln 268:   difference in wording.

ln 205   Ona III ln 245:   difference in wording.

ln 206   Ona III ln 177:   slight difference in word-
            ing.

ln 207   For "dust", cf. Ona III   ln 246.   For the
            full etymology given here, see Wutz, p. 263.

ln 208   Ona III   ln 180:   difference of wording.

ln 209   Ona III   ln 183:   there the form is "Zambri".

ln 210   Ona III   ln 187.

ln 211   Ona III   ln 188.

ln 212   Ona III   ln 189:   difference of wording.

ln 213   So Jerome, see Wutz, pp. 481 ff.   Contrast
            Ona III   ln 191.

ln 214   Ona III   ln 193:   difference of wording.

ln 215   Ona III ln 197: complete difference in
          wording.

ln 216   Cf. Ona III ln 208.

ln 217   Ona III ln 250: difference of wording.

ln 218   No parallels to the etymology are found in
          Wutz' materials.

ln 219   Ona III ln 253.

ln 220   Cf. Ona III ln 254; Ona I ln 391; Wutz,p.195.

ln 221   Ona III ln 256.

ln 222   The spelling "T'ap'or" (MS 55) is demanded
          by alphabetical order, although "T'abor"
          (MS 81) is more correct. See Ona III ln 248.

ln 223   Corrupt in both copies for "T'erap'im": see
          Ona III lns 259-260.

ln 224   The spelling restored is that apparently deman-
          ded by alphabetical order. The name occurs,
          with a different etymology, in Ona I ln 376.
          For etymology, cf. Wutz, p. 145, but there is
          no exact parallel. It derives doubtless from
          תבל .

ln 225   Ona III ln 261.

ln 226   No parallel to this name is found in Wutz, nor
          does it appear in Bible, unless it is corrupt.

ln 227   With certain hesitation, this resolution of
          the abbreviation is given. This abbreviation
          usually stands for "Israel". Here, however,
          it is apparently a corruption for Ἰεζραηλ
          which appears in Ona I ln 619 as 3ɓqɲwɓ[
          with the same etymology as here (see apparatus

criticus in loc.) and compare also Ona III
ln 417. A form such as *ḥɬqɲwɬɩ* would also
appear to be demanded by alphabetical order
at this point and "Israel" appears immediately
following here ln 231. No such etymology
appears in the abundant sources for "Israel"
quoted by Wutz, pp. 88-90.

ln 228   Cf. Ona III ln 267. The same strange rendering of "T'amar" as "branch", noted on ln 207
supra, recurs here. No parallels were found.

ln 229   Ona III ln 270: difference in wording.

ln 230   Ona III ln 271: note similar inclusion of
ɬ "is" in both lists, but difference in
wording.

ln 231   Ona III ln 274: difference in wording.

ln 232   For "seer of God", cf. Ona III ln 275. The
exact wording of the phrase occurs in Ona I
ln 414. For "vanquisher of God" no parallel
is to be found in all the material assembled
by Wutz. The etymology is drawn, of course,
from Gen 32:28.

ln 233   Ona III ln 347: difference in wording.

ln 234   Ona III ln 285.

ln 235   Ona III ln 286.

ln 236   Ona III ln 287: difference in wording.

ln 237   Ona III ln 320: This is the same item,
contrast Ona III ln 76.

ln 238   Ona III ln 288.

ln 239   Ona III ln 290.

ln 240   Ona III   ln 292.

ln 241   Ona III   ln 293.

ln 242   Ona III   ln 685.

ln 243   Ona III   ln 296.

ln 244   Ona III   ln 297:   difference in wording.

ln 245   The name is apparently missing from the mate-
           rial assembled by Wutz. It is, in fact, an
           Armenian word meaning "heap of stones". Com-
           pare Ona III   ln 110 Գալաադ. կարկառ վկայութեան
           "Galaad, heap (karkaṙ) of witness".

ln 246   Ona III   ln 298.

ln 247   Cf. Ona III   ln 300. Wutz' rendering of
           պանդխտութեան   as "consolationis" is bizarre.

ln 248   Ona III   ln 301.

ln 249   Ona III   ln 302.

ln 250   Ona III   ln 694.

ln 251   Ona III   ln 304.

ln 252   Ona III   ln 306.

ln 253   Alternatively "difficult":   cf. Ona III   ln 309
           with different wording.

ln 254   The spelling of the name in MS 81 accords with
           alphabetical order. The etymology given here
           may be compared with Ona III   ln 311 փառք ամի.
           "glory of all". The present reading appears
           to have arisen through inner-Armenian confusion
           of two abbreviations.

ln 255   Ona III   ln 308.

ln 256   Ona III   ln 310:   difference in wording.

ln 257   i.e. "Colossians"; or "of desire": Compare
          Ona III ln 313: the etymology there differs
          somewhat.

ln 258   Ona III ln 312: difference in wording.

ln 259   For "bald" compare Ona III ln 316, Ona I ln
          448. The other etymologies are to be found in
          Ona III ln 315, where the name is spelt
          "Kōrē" in Ona III, while the form "Korx" oc-
          curs in Ona I. In our text קרח and קרא have
          been combined.

ln 260   i.e. Armenia; the name "Ararat" and its ety-
          mology occur in Ona III lns 77-78. The form-
          ulation found here does not occur in the other
          Armenian lists.

ln 261   Ona III ln 331: this word disrupts the al-
          phabetical order.

ln 262   Ona III ln 327: wording is quite different.

ln 263   Ona III ln 328.

ln 264   i.e. India; there is no parallel to this name
          in the Armenian lists. It may be compared
          with Latin "Supher", which is, in one list,
          equivalent to "Ophir" in etymology: see Wutz,
          p. 467. It seems likely that the correct
          reading is "Ophir", but the corruption may be
          pre-Armenian. This word occurs in Ona I, ln
          674, Ona III ln 517. No possible basis for
          the etymology given by the list here suggests
          itself.

ln 265   i.e. Indians; cf. Ona III ln 269: The ety-
          mology derives from the Hebrew הודו which was,
          presumably, included at some stage of the
          transmission. In Ona III the name is transli-

terated.

ln 266   Ona III ln 337: wording is quite different.

ln 267   i.e. Rome; Ona III ln 556: the name in Ona
III is simply a transliteration of Latin and
the form *դերամբարծ* there is presumably corrupt.

ln 268   Ona III ln 554: difference in wording and
transliteration of the name.

ln 269   Ona III ln 278.

ln 270   Ona III ln 343.

ln 271   Ona III ln 341.

ln 272   Ona III ln 342: the name, in both manuscripts, appears in this form, not as "ṭapi-
dot'".

ln 273   Or "laws": cf. Ona III ln 284 *Լէ ūի· օրէն*
"Lēči.law".

ln 274   Ona III ln 344.

ln 275   The reading of MS 55 is corrupt, cf. Hebrew
לחי : Ona III ln 283: different wording.

ln 276   Ona III ln 345.

ln 277   A general resemblance to this reading may be
observed in Ona III ln 350, Ona I ln 499.

ln 278   Ona III ln 352.

ln 279   Here the spelling of MS 81 reflects the alphabetical order, which is, in fact, disturbed by
the intrusive -y- in ln 277. The name is
found in Ona III ln 354, but there the etymology is corrupt and, apparently also differs. That occuring here is not paralleled

by any of those cited by Wutz, p. 272, and its
connection with the root מע"ך is far from obvious.

ln 280   Ona III   ln 358.

ln 281   Ona III   ln 359:   the alphabetical order is
somewhat disturbed at this point.

ln 282   i.e. Magdalene;   Ona III   ln 357.

ln 283   The etymology does not appear in Wutz' materials.   It is obviously derived through the Hebrew root יק"ד so מוקד (Isa 33:14, PS 102:4,
etc.)

ln 284   Cf. Ona III   ln 360.

ln 285   This name is apparently a somewhat corrupt
form of Malaliēl,Ona I   ln 521, Ona III   ln
361.   The etymologies in both cases cited con-
cord with the present in sense, but not in
wording.

ln 286   Cf. Ona III   ln 365:   the name there is spelt
"Malak'ōn".

ln 287   Ona III   ln 366:   difference in wording.

ln 288   Ona III   ln 367 bears a general resemblance to
this etymology.

ln 289   Ona III   ln 368.

ln 290   Ona III   ln 369.

ln 291   Ona III   ln 370.

ln 292   Ona III   ln 377.

ln 293   Ona III   ln 392:   in Ona III the name is
"Misē".

ln 294   Ona III ln 372:   "Masep'at" Ona III;
           "Masep'ay" 55.

ln 295   Ona III ln 371.

ln 296   Ona III ln 376:   the alphabetical order indi-
           cates that both MSS are corrupt and should
           read "Matt'ēos.

ln 297   Ona III ln 379.

ln 298   Ona III ln 380.

ln 299   Ona III ln 386:   55 reads "king, lord".

ln 300   Ona III ln 387.

ln 301   Ona III ln 388.

ln 302   Cf. Ona III ln 399 "Mik'ōł".

ln 303   Ona III ln 395 "Mip'ibōsēt':   wording differs.

ln 304   Ona III ln 389.

ln 305   Cf. Ona III ln 390.   The etymology there ex-
           plains between which rivers this land is loca-
           ted.   In the present list, the Armenian trans-
           lation of "Mesopotamia" is given as the etymo-
           logy.

ln 306   Ona III ln 394:   the identification with Kad-
           ēs does not occur there;   see supra, ln 238.

ln 307-8   This and line 306 may be divergent forms of
           the same name.   With "Miłk'ay", cf. Ona I
           ln 545 "Melkea, queen";   ln 564 մեղիք
           "king".   Ln 308 is found in Ona III ln 396.
           Observe the graphic similarity of արքայ
           "king" and արքատ "poor" in uncial script.
           Note further that ln 307 disturbs the alphabe-
           tical order.

ln 309   Ona III   ln 397.

ln 310   Cf. Ona III   ln 393.

ln 311   Ona III   ln 398:   the text of our list is
            preferable.

ln 312   Ona III   ln 391.

ln 313   This presumably refers to a mena (measure),
            cf. Ona III   ln 400. Neither form of the word
            occurs in Ezek 38.

ln 314   Ona III   ln 401.

ln 315   The spelling of MS 55 is preferable: cf.
            Ona III   lns 402-403.   Two different words are
            involved   מצה and   משא .

ln 316   Ona III   ln 406:   different wording.

ln 317   Ona III   ln 357.

ln 318   So Ona I   ln 592:   contrast Ona III   ln 412.

ln 319   So Ona III   ln 264:   spelling of Ona III
            betrays transliteration.

ln 320   For the name, see Wutz, p. 779.   No parallels
            to the etymologies are obvious.   "Elevation"
            may derive from על and "goat of field" from
            אי   and איל .

ln 321   Ona III   ln 413.

ln 322   Ona III   ln 414.

ln 323   Ona III   ln 408.

ln 324   For the etymology "Jerusalem" compare Wutz,
            p. 723.   The word rendered "kicking" does not
            occur in the dictionaries, but is derived from
            a verb of this general meaning.   It should
            perhaps be compared with πεπατημένη (Origen,

apud Wutz, p. 745), and καταπατούμενος
(Wutz, p. 839) Ona III ln 416. These exact
etymologies do not occur in the other Armenian
lists.

ln 325   Ona III ln 334.

ln 326   This is apparent by a corrupt form of Ish-
Bosheth, cf. Ona III ln 272.

ln 327   Ona III ln 433.

ln 328   Cf. Ona III ln 430.

ln 329   Ona III lns 431-432.

ln 330   Ona III ln 4lb.

ln 331   Ona III ln 418: the etymology "offering" is
not found there. For it, see the texts quoted
by Wutz, pp. 774, 1023.

ln 332   Ona III ln 420.

ln 333   Ona III ln 426.

ln 334   This name not in Ona III: it occurs in Ona I
ln 611 with a different etymology. For that
given here, see Wutz, p. 255, etc.

ln 335   Ona III ln 434.

ln 336   Ona III ln 420.

ln 337   Ona III ln 428: different wording.

ln 338   Ona III ln 427.

ln 339   For "lamenter", MS 81 reads ωρρԵgoη "drinker",
perhaps an inner-Armenian variant: see Ona III
ln 450.

ln 340   Ona III ln 439.

ln 341   The word ρρшπш does not occur in the diction-
          aries. It is perhaps to be connected with the
          word ρρπιш "earth". This name occurs in Ona
          III ln 440 with a different etymology and
          there are no other clear parallels.

ln 342   Ona III ln 453.

ln 343   Ona III ln 441.

ln 344   Ona III ln 443.

ln 345   Ona III lns 444-445.

ln 346   The reading "Yovakim" of MS 81 is corrupt as
          is indicated by line 342 above where it occurs,
          by the alphabetical order which it disturbs
          and by the etymology itself. The etymology
          occurs in Ona III ln 427 for another form of
          this name "Yek'onias".

ln 347   Ona III ln 437.

ln 348   Cf. Ona III ln 451; "just" does not occur
          there, nor is it usual with this name. Compare
          ln 351 below.

ln 349   This and the following two names are only to
          be found in MS 55. With this, contrast Ona III
          ln 454 and see abbreviation above on ln 17.

ln 350   The incorrect "Yovnadan" of the MS has been
          emended: compare Ona III ln 455 with
          different wording.

ln 351   Compare this with ln 348, supra, these being
          variant forms of the same name.

ln 352   Ona III ln 456.

ln 353   Ona III ln 458.

ln 354   Ona III   ln 459.

ln 355   Ona III   ln 265:   wording differs.

ln 356   Not in the Armenian lists: compare the mater-
            ials in Wutz, p. 375, n.1.

ln 357   Ona III   ln 460.

ln 358   Ona III   ln 438.

ln 359   Ona III   ln 446:   more correct spelling
            "Yoak'az"   in Ona III.

ln 360   The form "Yewayim"   is doubtless corrupt for
            "Yewanim".   Contrast Ona III   ln 415.   No
            clear parallels occur in Wutz.   The etymology
            doubtless derives from the Hebrew root ינ"ה .

ln 361   See Ona III   ln 475:   This should probably be
            restored as Նասոն "Naason".

ln 362   Ona III   ln 462.

ln 363   Ona III   ln 463:   different wording.

ln 364   Ona III   ln 465:   the etymology "pit" is not
            found there, nor elsewhere in Wutz' materials.

ln 365   Ona III   ln 466:   different wording.

ln 366   Ona III   ln 471.

ln 367   Ona III   ln 472.

ln 368   Ona III   ln 473.

ln 369   Ona III   ln 474:   MS 55 adds "Nayin, god's
            offering",   a reading obviously conflated of
            lns 367-368.

ln 370   Cf. Ona III   ln 461:   from Hebrew נאים .
            Contrast Ona I for this word, derived from
            נעים.

ln 371   Ona I   ln 664.

ln 372   Ona III   ln 476.

ln 373   Compare the material assembled by Wutz, p.498,
           where analogous etymologies are found; for the
           name, see Ona III   ln 481.

ln 374   Ona III   ln 478.

ln 375   Ona III   ln 482.

ln 376   Ona III   ln 479.

ln 377   A name otherwise attested only in Latin, cf.
           Wutz, p. 329.

ln 378   Ona III   ln 483:   different wording.

ln 379   Ona III   ln 484.

ln 380   Ona III   ln 485.

ln 381   Ona III   lns 486-487:   different wording.

ln 382   Some corruption of Hebrew במדבר lies behind
           this reading. No parallels occur in Wutz.

ln 383   One III   ln 565-566.

ln 384   Ona III   ln 651.

ln 385   Ona III   ln 501.

ln 386   Ona III   ln 494.

ln 387   A similar name $\Omega_L{}_l \omega$ "Ula" (as in MS 81)   with
           this etymology does not appear in Wutz' mater-
           ials. It may perhaps be derived from חיל or
           איל .. More likely, however, is the view that
           it is an inner-Armenian corruption of $q > \iota_l$.
           In MS 55 $\Omega q \omega$ "Oza" is found, but there has
           been a hmt. which has resulted in the loss of
           the latter part of ln 385 plus the first part

of line 386. With this form, compare Ona III
ln 490.

ln 388   Cf. Ona III lns 490, 492.

ln 389   Ona III ln 493.

ln 390   Cf. Ona III ln 495: different wording.

ln 391   No ready parallels to this name can be observe... served in Wutz, nor does it appear in the
Bible.

ln 392   In MS 81 there is a corruption of η > η. The
reading of MS 55 shows its frequent shift of
η "d" to θ "t̓": Ona III ln 497.

ln 393   Ona III ln 499.

ln 394   Ona III ln 500.

ln 395   Ona III ln 703.

ln 396   Ona III ln 508.

ln 397   Ona III ln 512: MS 81 is corrupt.

ln 398   Corrupt form of the Hebrew name of this book.

ln 399   Ona III ln 515.

ln 400   The name does not appear in Ona III. In Ona I,
ln 685, it occurs with a different etymology.
For that here, cf. Ona III ln 90. It is found
in the material cited by Wutz, p. 517.

ln 401   Ona III ln 518: different wording.

ln 402   Ona III ln 521.

ln 403   Ona III ln 520.

ln 404   Ona III ln 530.

ln 405   Ona III ln 524.

ln 406   Ona III   ln 333.

ln 407   Cf. Ona III   ln 536 "Rabba".

ln 408   Ona III   ln 541.

ln 409   Ona III   ln 543:   different wording.

ln 410   Ona III   ln 535.

ln 411   Ona III   ln 544 "Ram".

ln 412   Ona III   ln 545.

ln 413   Ona III   ln 546.

ln 414   Ona III   ln 547.

ln 415   Ona I ln 705.

ln 416   Ona III ln 549

ln 417   Ona III   ln 551 and Ona I   ln 710 have this
            name, but each has an etymology different from
            the other, and both differ from that in the
            new list.   No parallels to the present etymo-
            logy may be found in Wutz.

ln 418   The name occurs in Ona III   ln 548 and other
            places (e.g. Wutz, pp. 92, etc.).   A possible
            alternative meaning for the word rendered
            "side" is "satiated", which might hesitantly
            be associated with Ona III ln 548 and the
            meaning multum accipiens, cf. Wutz, p. 469.

ln 419   The name occurs in Ona III   ln 552 with a
            different etymology.   A different sense of
            רכב   is behind Ona I   ln 713.   If Wutz n. on
            p. 986, is correct, the reading of Ona III
            ln 552 arises from an incorrect rendering of
            Latin quadriga.

ln 420   Ona III   ln 553.

ln 421   Ona III   ln 670:   different wording.

ln 422   Ona III   lns 558-559.

ln 423   Ona III   ln 560:   different wording.

ln 424   Saducees; Ona III   ln 574.

ln 425   Ona III   ln 577.

ln 426   Ona III   ln 578.

ln 427   Ona III   ln 579:   different wording.

ln 428   Ona III   ln 581.

ln 429   Ona III   ln 582:   different wording.

ln 430   Ona III   ln 587.

ln 431   The readings of MS 55 are to be preferred,
            particularly կրկնութիւն "repetition", for
            կրթութիւն "exercise" of 81:   Ona III ln 595.

ln 432   The etymologies offered by the MSS here do not
            occur in Arm I or III.   That of MS 55 եղեալ
            յԱստուծոյ "placed by God" is analogous to
            material found in Wutz, p. 116, derived from
            שים   and   אל .   No parallel to that of MS 81 is
            found.

ln 433   Ona III   lns 596-597.

ln 434   For "adversary", see Ona I   ln 771.   "Having
            borrowed" is not parallel and may go back to
            some corruption now beyond recovery.

ln 435   Ona III   ln 598.

ln 436   The word մակրղակ the etymology of "Sarona", is
            not found in the dictionaries.   For the name,
            see Ona III   ln 601.

ln 437   The reading *ưηι t̞ưɯ*   of MS 55 is an
          inner-Armenian corruption: Ona III lns 602 -
          603.

ln 438   Ona III ln 605: the reading *Uưɫưn* "Sap'ar"
          of Ona III is corrupt.

ln 439   Ona III 618.

ln 440   Ona III ln 627.

ln 441   Ona III ln 619.

ln 442   Ona III ln 606.

ln 443   Ona III ln 613 has the etymology "remaining",
          (using a different verb) and ln 621 has
          "peace-maker".

ln 444   Ona III ln 622.

ln 445   Cf. Ona I ln 747.

ln 446   Ona III ln 614.

ln 447   Ona III lns 624-625.

ln 448   This etymology is not recorded by Wutz. It
          derives, of course, from סנה and חרב.

ln 449   Ona III ln 630.

ln 450   Ona III lns 628-619: "Sēiōra" of Ona III
          ln 629 is corrupt.

ln 451   Ona III ln 610: Ona III does not have
          "sender".

ln 452   Ona III ln 632: different wording.

ln 453   Ona III ln 633.

ln 454   Ona III ln 640: different wording.

ln 455   Ona III ln 641.

ln 456   Ona III   lns 642-643.

ln 457   Ona III   ln 646:   different wording.

ln 458   Ona III   ln 644.

ln 459   Ona III   ln 645 reads ϑρι "number" which is,
              perhaps corrupt for ϑϐι "arm", a reading
              analogous to the present one, cf. Hebrew
              שכם.

ln 460   Ona III   ln 638.

ln 461   i.e. "Iscariot"; Ona III   ln 273.

ln 462   Ona III   ln 653.

ln 463   The spelling of MS 55, equivalent to Ona III
              ln 654, has been preserved.

ln 464   No parallels to this name or etymology appear.
              It is apparently derived from Latin somnus.

ln 465   Ona III   ln 648.

ln 466   Contrast Ona III   ln 655, which is a confused
              reading.

ln 467   Ona III   ln 652.

ln 468   No parallels are evident.

ln 469   Ona III   ln 255.

ln 470   Ona III   ln 661.

ln 471   Ona III   ln 662.

ln 472   Ona III   ln 663.

ln 473   Ona III   ln 664.

ln 474   Ona III   ln 666.

ln 475   Ona III   ln 671.

ln 476   The etymology is similar but not identical to
           those assembled by Wutz, p. 133.

ln 477   Ona III   ln 673.

ln 478   Ona III   ln 676.

ln 479   Ona III   lns 677-678.

ln 480   i.e. Pharisees; Ona III   ln 679.

ln 481   Ona III   ln 680:   different wording.

ln 482   Ona III   ln 684:   different wording.

ln 483   Compare Wutz, p. 430. Absent from Ona I, III.

ln 484   Ona I   ln 806:   different wording.

ln 485   Ona III   ln 685.

ln 486   The reading of MS 81 is clearly corrupt, cf.
           Ona I   850.   The etymology derives from כזב .

ln 487   Cf. Ona I   ln 831.

ln 488   Ona III   ln 686:   different wording.

ln 489   Ona III   ln 687.

ln 490   Ona III   ln 323:   for "friendship", MS 81
           reads բարեբանութիւն "praise, benediction".

ln 491   Ona III   ln 303, cf. Ona II ln 45.

ln 492   Ona III   ln 338.

ln 493   Ona III   ln 339.

ln 494   Cf. Ona I   ln 835.

ln 495   Ona III   ln 697.

ln 496   Cf. Ona III   ln 335.

ln 497   Ona III   ln 698.

VI

ONA VI

i. Sample of Forty Names

1. Աբբանայ. քար որոց երկրպագէ ին կամ կոոց տուն կամ
                     բաղա լիք կամ լուացման տեղիք:

2. Աբբոր. պա հանորդ:

3. Արղլմեհ. ծառայ քրիստոսի:

4. Աբեդայ. սզաւոր կամ տեւաւոր:

5. Աբիան. աղբատ:

6. Աբրայ. բարկացումն:

7. Ազապէն. սիրուն:

8. Ազապ. սէր:

9. ազա հ. անյազ:

10. Ազաթանգեղոս. բարի հրեշտակ:

11. Ազաթիմովթ. նղենի խլեւլ {marg քք}:

12. ազարակ. անղ կամ փոքր գիւղ:

13. ազանել. օթեվանիլ կամ զզենուլ:{marg հ}

14. Ազազ. երինչք:

15. ազատութիւն. կոչումն:

16. Ազանովթայ. անoթ երաժշտի կամ գործի:

17. Ազղէն. թիլրաղարծ:

18. ազելոյն. հազնելոյ յոտս:

19. Ազոն. մրցութեան հրահանգ:

20. ազորանք. մթերք աղբոյ:

1. Abbanay,   a stone which they worshipped, or house
                 of idols or ⌠   ⌡ or places of
                 ⌠   ⌡.

2. Abbor,   guard.

3. Abdlmseh,   servant of Christ.

4. Abełay,   mournful or black.

5. Abian,   poor.

6. Abray,   anger.

7. Agapēn,   lovable.

8. Agap,   love.

9. Agah,   avaricious.

10. Agat'angełos, good angel.

11. Agat'ŕimovt', uprooted pomegranate tree {marg:
                 trees}

12. Agarak,   field or small village.

13. Aganel,   to lodge or to dress.

14. Agag,   heifer.

15. Agasut'iwn, call.

16. Aganovt'ay, instrument of music or work.

17. Agdēn,   false return.

18. Ageloyn,   of putting on the feet.

19. Agon,   instruction in wrestling.

20. Agorank',   heaps of dung.

21. Ազոր.   պաՀանորդ կամ բարձրութիւն:

22. Ազունիա.   ծածուկ:

23. ագւտ.   զոզ կամ ադաբողոն:

24. Աղամայ.   եւ սիրոյ իմոյ ի Ե. քաղաքացն
                         սողոմայ:

25. Ադին.   ուրախութիւն կամ փափկութիւն:

26. Ադիալիպտոս. անձանձրոյթ:

27. Ադոնա.   տէր կամ ամէնակալ:

28. {[Ադ]ոնայի.   տէր բսի յ[եբր]այեցի լեզուն:}

29. Ադոն.   տէր կամ ենթակա կամ տանաւղ կամ խարիսխ:

30. Ադոնիայի.   տեառն իմոյ կամ Թուոյ յոլովութիւն
                         մի է յանուանց ատտուծոյ զոր երբեմն
                         եդ փոխանակ անուան Աստուծոյ
                         որ չորիւք բաղկանայ
                         տառիւք:

31. Ադարմեղեկի. . . .

32. Ադոնմոյ.   պարզ բառ:

33. ագազուն.   նուազ կամ տղեղ:

34. ՞ագգ.   սեռ կամ ցեղ:

35. ագղող.   ուժեղ:

36. ագղր.   անդամ:

37. ագղեր.   Թեզանի:

38. Ագղեովթ.   ձոր կամ ցամաք:

39. Ագեկայ.   արեգակն:

40. Ագմուղեւ.   չար դեւ:

21. Agor,   guard or height.

22. Agunia,   hidden.

23. Aguṙ,   hollow, or cloak.

24. Adamay,   and of my love; (one) of the five
                   cities of Sodom.

25. Adin,   joy, or delight.

26. Adialeptos,   indefagitable.

27. Adona,   lord, or omnipotent.

28. {[Ad]onayi,   lord is (thus) heard in the [He]brew
                   tongue.}

29. Adon,   lord, or subject, or bearer, or base.

30. Adoniayi,   of my lord, or plural in number. It is
                   one of the names of God which some-
                   times it (i.e. scripture) places in-
                   stead of the name of God which is com-
                   posed of four letters.

31. Adarmeɫeki,   . . .

32. Adonmoy,   simple word.

33. Azazun,   few, or ugly.

34. Azg,   generation, or tribe.

35. Azdoɫ,   strong.

36. Azdr,   limb.

37. Azder,   sleeve.

38. Azdēovt',   valley, or dry land.

39. Azeka,   sun.

40. Azmoldew,   bad demon.

1   որոց } որ | բաղանիք | լուցման տեղիք   4

Աբեղա   5   Աբիոն   9   om   10   ազարակք

13   օթեւանիլ   14   ազատութիւնք կոչունք   16   om

18   om   19   հրահանք   20   աղբից   24   om

25   փափկութիւն կամ ուրախութիւն   27   կամ }   om

28   om   29   om   30   om   31   Աղրամէլիք

արբայութիւն   35   ազղուօղ   38   ազտէովղ

40

ln 1   MS 64 ln 3:   the end is corrupt for *բաղանացիք*
         կամ լուացման տեղիք

         (MS 64 and One I ln 78). No parallels to the
         first part of the etymology occur in Wutz, but
         perhaps a derivation from אבן is involved.

ln 2   MS 64 ln 4;   the name does not occur in any of
         Wutz' lists nor is the etymology readily ex-
         plicable.

ln 3   MS 64 ln 8;   this is clearly the name and
         etymology of Ona III ln 7 which has been mis-
         read by Wutz as "Abdlmoeh". He has not trans-
         lated the unmistakable *քի*.as "of Christ".

ln 4   MS 64 ln 10;   Ona I ln 105 has "Abeła, mourn-
         ing." No parallel to "black" appears and,
         incidentally, the form of the word is not
         listed in the dictionaries.

ln 5   MS 64 ln 16;   Ona III ln 12.

ln 6   MS 64 ln 26;   Ona I ln 110. The same word
         appears with a different etymology in Ona III.

ln 7   MS 64 ln 30;   the form "Agapos" occurs in Ona
         I and III, each with a different etymology and
         not derived from the Greek stem invoked by MS
         64 and Ona VI. No other parallels are quoted
         by Wutz.

ln 8   MS 64 ln 31;   the comments in the preceding
         note also apply to this item.

ln 9   MS 64 omits.

ln 10   MS 64 ln 32;   not in Wutz or the Bible.

ln 11   MS 64 ln 34;   Ona I ln 81 with different word-
         ing.

ln 12   MS 64 ln 33.

ln 13   MS 64 ln 35.

ln 14   MS 64 ln 36;   Ona I ln 17 apparatus, Ona II
           ln 9.

ln 15   MS 64 ln 37;   the word ազատութիւն a clearly
           Armenian formation, does not appear in the
           dictionaries.

ln 16   Not in MS 64 nor in Wutz. The word is drawn
           from LXX Isa. 42:24. The form quoted is
           actually an Armenian oblique case, the way
           the word appears in the Armenian version of
           Isaiah. It reflects Hebrew אגנות .

ln 17   MS 64 ln 40;   The name is not found in Wutz
           or the Bible. The word given as an etymology
           is not found in any of the dictionaries, but
           is compounded of two known elements. S. Shaked
           has suggested that this might conceivably re-
           flect Pahlavi agdēn "impious", if "difficult
           return" could be interpreted eschatologically.

ln 18   MS 64 omits.

ln 19   MS 64 ln 42;   like items 7 and 8, this is a
           Greek word not found in Wutz' onomastic mater-
           ial.

ln 20   MS 64 ln 41;   this is a variant spelling of
           the word agořank'.

ln 21   MS 64 ln 45;   On the form, see Wutz, p. 959 n.
           where an original *Argob is suggested. The
           form occurring here is found elsewhere with
           the etymology "height", see Ona I, p. 864
           apparatus, Ona II ln 7. "Guard" is identical
           with the insoluble name "Abbor" in ln 2, above,
           and perhaps a graphic confusion and conflation

of readings are possible.

ln 22   MS 64 ln 44; the name is without parallel
        and quite inexplicable.

ln 23   MS 64 ln 43; the connection is apparently
        between the sense of <u>agut</u> "hollow of hand"
        and the sense of <u>gog</u> "hollow, cavity". The
        relationship with <u>ałaboron</u> "cloak" is quite
        obscure.

ln 24   MS 64 omits. The reference is to Adma אדמה
        mentioned with Sodom and three other cities
        in Gen 10:19. The etymology, however, may
        be derived from the stem חמ"ד reflected in
        the name חמדן which, metathesized as
        is the translation in LXX Gen 36:36 (contrast
        <u>L</u> ἁμαδα): cf. Wutz, p. 895 n. A striking
        example.

ln 25   MS 64 ln 51; the etymology "delight" occurs
        in Ona I, p. 866 apparatus. "Joy" is not
        found elsewhere.

ln 26   MS 64 ln 52; deriving from Greek ἀδιάλειπτος .
        Occurs six times in the LXX and six times in
        the NT. No particular reason for its selec-
        tion for transliteration can be seen.

ln 27   MS 64 ln 54; See Ona I ln 74, Ona III ln 29,
        Ona V ln 28 for the name and the etymology
        "lord". The reading "omnipotent" appears to
        be expansionary in character like the read-
        ings in items 4 and 25.

ln 28   MS 64 ln 64; a marg. note <u>secunda</u> <u>manu</u>. The
        etymology "lord" is more usually found for
        "Adon", so Ona I lns 74-75, Ona III lns 29-30
        Ona V lns 28-29. No clear parallel to the

gloss is found, but cf. ln 30.

ln 29   MS 64 omits. For the etymology, see Ona III
ln 29.

ln 30   MS 64 omits; see Ona III ln 30 which also
contain the gloss, except for the final
phrase.

ln 31   MS 64 ln 59; for the name, see Ona I ln 71,
and MS 64 has just the first word of the etymology given by Ona I. Ona VI omits the etymology and the form of the name seems corrupt.
In the dictionary of Eremia vardapet only the
name "Adarmeheki" is found. This is doubtless to be related to Ararmeliki. The etymology given these resembles that given by
Ona I for "Adam".

ln 32   MS 64 ln 55; this name is listed in Wutz'
Index s.v. but does not occur in his text.
Might it be corrupt for "Adovnoy" and does
the strange etymology mean that it is singular as opposed to the plural on ln 30?

ln 33   MS 64 ln 61; the basic meaning of this word
is "dried up, withered" which is apparently
extended to the meanings given here.

ln 34   MS 64 ln 68.

ln 35   MS 64 ln 69.

ln 36   MS 64 ln 70.

ln 37   MS 64 ln 71; H. Ačaryan in his etymological
dictionary of the Armenian language, s.v.
quotes the apparently identical Ազգիր known
only from the dictionary of Eremia vardepet
with this same meaning. See: Armenian Ety-

mological Dictionary, Vol. I, Erevan: 1971,
(in Armenian), but on the meaning of the witness, see: Introductory Remarks, supra.

ln 38   MS 64 ln 72;   no clear origin for the name or
its etymology was found.

ln 39   MS 64 ln 73;   the name occurs with quite a
different etymology in Wutz, p. 358 et al.

ln 40   MS 64 omits;   The name is most probably corrupt for Ազմոդեւ "Azmodew", i.e. Asmodeus
(A suggestion of N. Bogharian).

ii. Sample of letter "ben"

1. Բաբայ.　　　բլուր:

2. Բաէլ.　　　մանաւոր կամ խառնակութիւն:

3. Բաալ.　　　կուռք կամ տիրող:

4. Բաադ.　　　պատերազմեցաւ Աստուած:

5. Բաադիմ.　　կուռք տիրողք:

6. Բաբելոն.　　փոփոխումն կամ բաբել կամ խոռվութիւն
　　　　　　　　կամ խառնակութիւն բաբախել բախբախել:

7. Բաթուէդ.　　սիրելի աստուծոյ կամ զօրաւոր կամ
　　　　　　　　որդիութիւն աստուծոյ կամ դուստր
　　　　　　　　աստուծոյ կամ կոյս:

8. Բաթ.　　　միայն:

ln 1　　　No parallels are evident.

ln 2　　　Perhaps corrupt for Babēl for which Ona V ln
　　　　　93 has "confusion". No explanation for
　　　　　"partial" can be seen.

ln 3　　　Ona V ln 85.

ln 4　　　Perhaps a corrupt remnant of an etymology for
　　　　　a name such as Jerubaal.

ln 5　　　Not in agreement with Ona I ln 165. It con-
　　　　　cords with Ona III ln 96 with some difference
　　　　　in wording.

1. Babay   hill.

2. Baēl,   partial, or mixture.

3. Baal,   idol, or master.

4. Baaɫ,   god fought.

5. Baaɫim,   idols, masters.

6. Babelon,   change, or Babylon, or confusion,

                       or mixture, to palpitate, to palpi-

                       tate.

7. Bat'ueɫ   beloved of god, or general, or

                       sonship of god, or daughter of god,

                       or virgin.

8. Bat',   alone.

ln 6   "Change --- mixture" are drawn from Ona I ln
            130 apparatus. There follow two spellings of
            a word "to palpitate" for which etymology
            there are no known parallels.

ln 7   "Daughter --- virgin" are drawn from Ona I ln
            132 apparatus, cf. ln 185. In MS 55 of Ona V
            "sonship of God" is to be found. "Beloved of
            god or general" remain unexplained.

ln 8   Ona I ln 187.

VII

List of Manuscripts

1. Codex Ticinensis (Pavia), II 2, 12 cent.
                                    (Wutz, 849)

2. Berlin, Petermann 145, fols. 3r-33v, 1602
                      (Wutz, 849; Karamianz, no. 79)

3. Berlin, Minutius 273, fols. 2r-17v, 1618
                      (Wutz, 849; Karamianz, no. 80)

4. Vienna, Mechitarist no. 337, fols. 137r-158r, 15
   cent.   (Wutz, 849)

5. Paris, Bibliothèque Nationale, MS Arm 302, fols.
   79-93r, 13 cent.   (Wutz, 849)

6. Paris, Bibliothèque Nationale, MS Arm 271, fols.
   111v-119v, 17 cent.   (Wutz, 849)

7. Paris, Bibliothèque Nationale, MS Arm 260, fols.
   1-32r, 16 cent.   (Wutz, 849)

8. Vienna, Bibl. Aul. Cod. Arm., fols. 108r-118v, 1683
                                    (Wutz, 849)

9. Vienna, Mechitarist, no. 319, fols. 312v-325v, 1697
                                    (Wutz, 962)

10. Erevan, Matenadaran, no. 2371, Surxat', 1357
                                    (Catalogue 1,789)

11. Erevan, Matenadaran, no. 4149, Erznka, 1304-05
                                    (Catalogue 1,1157)

12. Erevan, Matenadaran, no. 5596, 13 cent.
                                    (Catalogue 2,141)

13. Erevan, Matenadaran, no. 5925, Varag (?), 15 cent.
                                    (Catalogue 2,213)

14. Erevan, Matenadaran, no. 8198, 14 cent.
                                    (Catalogue 2,693)

15. Erevan, Matenadaran, no. 266, 1468
                                    (Catalogue 1,285)

16. Erevan, Matenadaran, no. 267, 1609, 1613
(Catalogue 1,285-6)

17. Erevan, Matenadaran, no. 516, 17 cent.
(Catalogue 1,338-9)

18. Erevan, Matenadaran, no. 530, Jagavank', 14 cent.
(Catalogue 1,342)

19. Erevan, Matenadaran, no. 534, 17 cent.
(Catalogue 1,343)

20. Erevan, Matenadaran, no. 536, 17 cent.
(Catalogue 1,343)

21. Erevan, Matenadaran, no. 538, 1595
(Catalogue 1,343-4)

22. Erevan, Matenadaran, no. 843, Toxat', 18 cent.
(Catalogue 1,423)

23. Erevan, Matenadaran, no. 2019, Julfa, 1600
(Catalogue 1,701)

24. Erevan, Matenadaran, no. 2291, Caesaria, 1665
(Catalogue 1,768)

25. Erevan, Matenadaran, no. 2330, Kaffa, 1633, 1641-43
(Catalogue 1,776-7)

26. Erevan, Matenadaran, no. 2331, 17 cent.
(Catalogue 1, 777)

27. Erevan, Matenadaran, no. 2335, Jerusalem, 1476
(Catalogue 1, 779)

28. Erevan, Matenadaran, no. 2369, Constantinople, 1614
(Catalogue 1, 788)

29. Erevan, Matenadaran, no. 2370, Constantinople,
1621-24   (Catalogue 1,788-9)

30. Erevan, Matenadaran, no. 2372, 16 cent.
(Catalogue 1, 789)

31. Erevan, Matenadaran, no. 2381, Yovhannavank', 1631
(Catalogue 1, 791)

32. Erevan, Matenadaran, no. 3170, 17 cent.
                                  (Catalogue 1,955)

33. Erevan, Matenadaran, no. 3197, 16 cent.
                                  (Catalogue 1,961)

34. Erevan, Matenadaran, no. 3200, 17 cent.
                                  (Catalogue 1,962)

35. Erevan, Matenadaran, no. 3201, St. James, 1419
                                  (Catalogue 1,962)

36. Erevan, Matenadaran, no. 3202, 1417
                                  (Catalogue 1,962)

37. Erevan, Matenadaran, no. 3261, 17 cent.
                                  (Catalogue 1,975)

38. Erevan, Matenadaran, no. 3937, 1370
                                  (Catalogue 1,1114)

39. Erevan, Matenadaran, no. 4283, 1616(?)
                                  (Catalogue 1,1184)

40. Erevan, Matenadaran, no. 4398, 17 cent.
                                  (Catalogue 1,1205)

41. Erevan, Matenadaran, no. 5008, Tak'irdat, 1623-43
                                  (Catalogue 2,15)

42. Erevan, Matenadaran, no. 5919, 14 cent.
                                  (Catalogue 2,211)

43. Erevan, Matenadaran, no. 5947, 17 cent.
                                  (Catalogue 2,217-8)

44. Erevan, Matenadaran, no. 5995, 17 cent.
                                  (Catalogue 2,228-9)

45. Erevan, Matenadaran, no. 6624, 17 cent.: according
     to Amalyan (p. 234) this contains the work,
     but it is not listed in the contents in
     Catalogue 2, 359-60.

46. Erevan, Matenadaran, no. 7014, Jerusalem, 17 cent.
                                  (Catalogue 2,440-1)

47. Erevan, Matenadaran, no. 7117, Mecop', 1440 (?)
                              (Catalogue 2,464-5)

48. Erevan, Matenadaran, no. 7995, Istambul, 1632-3
                              (Catalogue 2,651)

49. Erevan, Matenadaran, no. 8106, 16 cent.
                              (Catalogue 2,674-5)

50. Erevan, Matenadaran, no. 8354, 17 cent.
                              (Catalogue 1,727)

51. Erevan, Matenadaran, no. 8563, Constantinople, 1620
                              (Catalogue 2,772)

52. Erevan, Matenadaran, no. 1921, 1732-3
                              (Catalogue 2,874)
     erroneously listed by Amlyan as no. 9112

53. Venice, Mechitarist, no. 1409, pp. 1-26, notragir

54. Venice, Mechitarist, no. 544, 14-15 cent., pp.1-30
     bolorgir

55. Venice, Mechitarist, no. 545, 16-17 cent., pp.393-
     404

56. Venice, Mechitarist, no. 39, pp. 120-137, notragir

57. Jerusalem, Armenian Patriarchate, no. 657, fols.
           285r-343v, notragir (Catalogue 3, 86-8)

58. Jerusalem, Armenian Patriarchate, no. 857, fols.
           101r-121v, notragir (Catalogue 3,348-9)

59. Jerusalem, Armenian Patriarchate, no. 1004, fols.
           2r-29r, 1613, notragir (Catalogue 4,6-7)

60. Jerusalem, Armenian Patriarchate, no. 1173, fols.
           3r-30v, 17 cent.   (Catalogue 4,272)

61. Jerusalem, Armenian Patriarchate, no. 1666, fols.
           97r ff., 1642   (Catalogue 5, 5)

62. Jerusalem, Armenian Patriarchate, no. 1672, pp. 5
           ff., 17 cent.   (Catalogue 5,527)

63. Jerusalem, Armenian Patriarchate, no. 1682, pp. 185
    ff., 1359   (Catalogue 5,543)

64. Jerusalem, Armenian Patriarchate, no. 1352, pp.297-
    504, Jerusalem, 1688   (Catalogue 4,625)

65. Jerusalem, Armenian Patriarchate, no. 2481, pp.122-
    149, 1306   (Catalogue 8,151)

66. Paris, Bibliothèque Nationale cod. arm. 140, fols.
    239v ff., notragir

67. Bzommar, no. 204, fols. 252v-260v, 1178
                                (Catalogue 1, 486-495)

68. Bzommar, no. 227, fols. 173r-196r, 1410
                                (Catalogue 1, 539-42)

69. Galata, no. 95 pp. 201-2 (alphabet)(Catalogue, 602)

70. Galata, no. 100, pp. 355-381, notragir
                                (Catalogue, 630)

71. Tabriz, no. II 14 (alphabet, some names) 1678
                                (Catalogue, 57)

72. Vienna, Mechitarist, no. 672, fols. 93r-121v,17 cent.
                                (Catalogue 2, 166)

73. Vienna, Mechitarist, no. 1017, fols. 2r-16r, 17-18
    cent.   (Catalogue 2, 608)

74. Vienna, Mechitarist, no. 1124, fols. 188r-191v, 18
    cent.   (Catalogue 2,768-9)

75. London, British Library, MS or 6991, fols. 141-220,
    18 cent.   (Catalogue, 311)

76. London, British Library, catalogue no. 260, fols.
    1r-31r, 16 cent.   (Catalogue, 137)

77. Oxford, Bodleian Library, MS or e 27, fol. 194, 18
    cent.   (Catalogue, 758)

78. Jerusalem, Armenian Patriarchate, no. 1372, pp. 29-
    59   (Catalogue 5, 8-10)

79. Jerusalem, Armenian Patriarchate, no. 1008, pp.1-15
                              (Catalogue 4, 11)

80. Jerusalem, Armenian Patriarchate, no. 1912,Kaffa(?),
    1369   (Catalogue 6,344)

81. Erevan, Matenadaran, no. 2261, fols. 300v-310v, 17
    cent.   (Catalogue 1,758)

82. Jerusalem, Armenian Patriarchate, no. 1422, fols.
    325r-613v, 17 cent.   (Catalogue 5, 86)

83. Jerusalem, Armenian Patriarchate, no. 1448, fols.
    263r-310r, 1583   (Catalogue 5, 129)

84. Jerusalem, Armenian Patriarchate, no. 1699, pp.
    10-69, 17 cent.   (Catalogue 5, 574)

85. Bzommar, no. 549, fols. 15 ff., 16-17 cent.
                              (Catalogue 2, 157)

86. Aleppo, 40 Martyrs, no. 72, pp. 5-48, 16 cent.
                              (Catalogue, 152)

87. New Julfa, All-Saviour, no. 75, fols. 4f-33v, 1220
                              (Catalogue, 837)

88. New Julfa, All-Saviour, no. 160, fols. 275-465,
    16-17 cent.   (Catalogue, 838)

89. Kurdian Collection, 18 century (Catalogue, 12)

90. Jerusalem, Armenian Patriarchate, no. 2523, pp.
    275-384, 17-18 cent. (Catalogue 8,199)

PART THREE

THE SONS OF NOAH

AND

THE GENERATIONS FROM ADAM

INTRODUCTORY REMARKS

The Peoples of the Sons of Noah

This text is based, ultimately, on Gen 10,2 Chr
1:5-21, both texts dealing with the enumeration of the
nations descending from the three sons of Noah and the
division of the earth among them. Other ancient sources
reflecting this tradition are, e.g. Jub. 7:13-19, Bib.
Ant. 4:1-10.

The document published here is drawn from Erevan,
MS No. 533, written in 1660 C.E. (Erevan Catalogue, 1,
cols. 342-43). It is particularly close to the material
parallel in content to be found in the Armenian version
of The Chronicle of Michael the Syrian. [1] A close parallel is also to be observed in the Syriac text of The
Chronicle. [2] An earlier stage of this tradition is to
be observed in The Cave of Treasures. [3]

A much expanded form of the same body of material,
in the section dealing with the descendants of Japheth,
may be observed in the second chapter of The History of
the Caucasian Albanians by Moses Dasxuranc'i. [4] In a
note to this passage, Dowsett points out that in it
Dasxuranc'i is dependent on the Chronicle by Hippolytus
which was published, in its Armenian version, by Sarghissian. [5] Chabot does not reckon Hippolytus' Chronicle among the sources used by Michael the Syrian, [6] and
a particularly close relationship exists between Michael's work and the text published here, as is indicated
at a number of points in the Commentary below. It thus
seems that there may be some intermediate link in the
transmission.

The Generations from Adam
      This is a chronological list by rulers, starting
from Adam and extending to the seventh century C.E. The
first figure following each name in this list indicates
the number of years which the designated person reigned.
The second of the two figures is a cumulative total. The
biblical ages generally follow the Septuagint reckoning,
where this differs from that of the massoretic text.
There are fairly frequent confusions and corruptions of
the numbers which have been signalled in the commentary
and, where possible, corrected in the text. In the
translation, the names have been given in their usual
English form where they could be clearly identified.
Unusual forms in Armenian are noted in the commentary.
      The work is found in Erevan, Matenadaran, No.8076,
fols. 221r–222r. This is a Miscellany of the 17th century, containing a good number of texts of interest for
study of the Pseudepigrapha. The Generations is not
listed by the Catalogue (Erevan Catalogue, 2. cols. 667-
668) and is followed by two pages of chronological sum-
maries which are not of great interest.
      The transliterations of names make it likely that
the list was translated into Armenian from Greek, and
such forms as Eɫisabos (ln 83),Iyovhannēs (lns 85,97),
the various corruptions of the name Onias (lns 87,90,93,
95), Ïesus (ln 94), and others all reflect Greek spelling rather than the usual Armenian forms of the names.
      From its conclusion it is likely that the list was
composed in the middle of the seventh century C.E.;
Heraclius ruled from 610-641 (see ln 154) and was succeeded by his two sons, first Heraclius Constantinus,
the "Constantinus" of The Generations (ln 155), who
ruled for some months, and then Heracleonas who was
immediately overthrown by the army. Next ruled Constans
II (642-688), apparently the "Kostandin" of the text
(ln 156.) The Generations from Adam records only two

years for his reign seemingly implying that it was completed in his third year, i.e. 644 C.E.

Էջ 234 ԱԶԳ ՈՐԴՈՑՆ ՆՈՅԻ

1 ի Սեմայ: եբրայեցիք· փռանկք· պարսիկք

եւ այլք:

Եւ է սահման Սեմայ: ընդ

Էջ 235 մէջ ջերկրեայս / յարեւելից եւ

յարեւմիցս. զպարսից աշխարհն·

զասորոց. զպաղեստին· մինչեւ՛ի

նեղոս գետ:

2 Յաբեդի ազգք: ՛հայք.

մակեդոնացիք· մաղացիք. յոյնք.

լատինացիք· ալանք· եւ վրացիք: Եւ

սահմանք յաբեդի է: մաղիէ մինչ

ի զադիրոն ՛հիւսխոյ.

եւ արդ ունի ազգն աբեդի

⟨յազեան⟩ տիգրիս գետոյ

որ բաժանէ ընդ մադէ եւ ընդ պարսս:

3 Քամայ են: եգիպտացիք· ՛հնդկացիք·

՛հեթացիք· յեփուսացիք· ՛հաբաշիք՝

որք են քուշացիք· ամուրՙհացիք·

զերզեսացիք· արուդացիք· քաղդէացիք

որք են ասորիք:

Եւ սահման քամայ է: զ՛հարաւ.

եւ մանիտոն էառ յայն կոյս

The People(s) of the Sons of Noah

1 <u>From Shem</u>: the Hebrews, the Franks, the

Persians and others.

And the border of Shem is around the

middle part of the earth, to the east and

to the west; the land of the Persians,

that of the Syrians, Palestine as far

as the river Nile.

2 <u>The Nations of Japheth</u>: the Armenians, the

Macedonians, the Medes, the Greeks, the

Latins, the Alans and the Georgians. And

the border of Japheth is from Media to

Northern Gadiron;

and now the nation of Japheth holds

⌐one word⌐   of the Tigris river

which is between Media and Persia.

3 <u>Of Ham are</u>: the Egyptians, the Indians, the

Hittites, the Jebusites, the Habašites

who are the Cušites, the Amorites, the

Gergasites, the Arudites, the Chaldaeans

who are the Syrians.

And the border of Ham is to the south,

and he took Manitōn on the other side

ծովուն:

4 Յետ աւետեացն աստուծոյ առ աբրահամ

ՆԼ ամ լինի մինչ ի յելսն յեգիպտոսէ.

ՄԲ մինչ ի գալն յակոբայ էր

եւ ՄԻԲ մինչեւ

ի յելսն. բայց ճՒՔ ամ ի

չարչարանս կային:

of the sea.

4 After the announcement of God to Abraham, there

were 430 years up to the exodus from Egypt.

There were 205 years up to the coming of

Jacob (i.e. to Egypt) and 225 (from that

time) until the exodus, but they were af-

flicted for 144 years.

---

1 եբրայեցիք "the Hebrews": The list of peoples resembles that of The Chronicle, but that work places the
"Syrians" first. Contrast here 3 below.

մէջ. "the middle part of the earth". The idea is not
present in The Chronicle, but compare The Cave of
Treasures "und ihnen gehört der Mittelpunkt der Erde".

2 *Հայք* "the Armenians": The Armenian version of The
Chronicle also places the Armenians first. They are
second in the Syriac.

Գադիրոն "Gadiron": So also Michael in The Chronicle,
and Dasxuranc'i. Dowsett identifies it as Cadiz, and
Chabot as Cadix. It is north of Media.

յազեան ʿone word⟩: Apparently corrupt. The Armenian
version of The Chronicle has *յակնէն* apparently a
mediaeval form for classical *յակաւնէն*"from the source
of", while in Dasxuranc'i the sentence reads "from
Media to Gadiron (Cadiz) in the north and down to the
river Tigris which separates Media from Babylon" (tr.
Dowsett, p.1). The Tigris, in fact, runs from Media
and Babylon, as stated by Dasxuranc'i; the reading
"Persia" of our text and The Chronicle is an important
indication of their affiliation.

3 *բադդեացիք* "Chaldeans": The Chaldeans and Syrians
appear in The Chronicle among the descendants of Shem,
see also Gen 10:22.

Ման իաոն--ծովուն "Maniton--sea": Quite inexplicable on
the basis of The Chronicle.

4 This chronology is standard. The period of 430
years is found in Exod 12:40, cf. Gal 3:17. Dating
by the promise to Abraham may be observed in The
Chronicle, Chabot pp. 35 ff., but The Chronicle reckons
215 years from the descent into Egypt to the Exodus (p.
39) and its ages for Isaac and Jacob also produce this
total for the period from the promise to Abraham up to
the Exodus.

ԾՆՈՒՆԴՔ ՅԱԴԱՄԱՅ ԵՒ ԹԻՒՔ ՆՈՑԱ

221ա 1　Ադամ եկաց ՄԼ ամ եւ ծնաւ զՍէթ:

Սէթ. ամս　　　ՄԵ միաւորեաւ եւ լինի ՆԼԵ:

Ենովս　　　ՑՂ　　　ՈԻԵ:

Կայինայն　　　ՑՀ　　　2ՂԵ:

5　Մաղաղիէլ　　　ՑԿԵ　　　ՋԿ:

Յարեթ　　　ՑԿԲ　　　ՈՑԻԲ:

Ենովք　　　ՑԿԵ　　　ՈՄՂԵ:

Մաթուսաղայ　　　ՑԿԵ　　　ՈՒՁԲ:

Ղամէք　　　ՑԲ　　　ՈՈԼՂ:

10　Նոյ　　　Ց　　　ՍՑԼՂ:

Սեմ　　　Ց　　　ՍՄԼՂ:

Արփաքսադ　　　ՑԼԷ　　　ՍՅՀՍ:

Կայինան　　　ՑԼ　　　ՍՑՍ:

Սաղայ　　　ՑԼ　　　ՍՈԼՍ:

15　Եբեր　　　ՑԼՂ　　　ՍՋԿԵ:

Փաղեկ　　　ՑԼ　　　ՍՊՂ

Ռագաւ　　　ՑԼԲ　　　ՍՋԻԷ:

Սերուք　　　ՑԼ　　　ՎԿԷ:

Նաքովր　　　ՀԹ　　　ՎՑԼՋ:

20　Թարայ　　　Հ　　　ՎՄՋ:

Աբրամ　　　Ց　　　ՎՅՋ:

Իսահակ　　　Կ　　　ՎՆՀԲ:

THE GENERATIONS FROM ADAM AND THEIR NUMBERS

1   Adam lived 230 years and begot Seth

Seth   205, altogether   435

Enosh   190   625

Kenan   170   795

5   Mahalalel 165   960

Jared   162   1,122

Enoch   165   1,29<7>

Methuselah 165   1,452

Lamech   102   1,634

10 Noah   500   2,134

Shem   100   2,234

Arpachshad 137   2,371

Kainan   130   2,501

Shelah   130   2,631

15 Eber   134   2,765

Peleg   130   2,89<5>

Reu   132   2,927

Serug   130   3,067

Nahor   79   3,136

20 Terah   70   3,206

Abraham   100   3,306

Isaac   60   3,472

Յակոբ	ՁԵ	ՎՇԾԲ:
Ղեւի	ԽՋ	ՎԿԵ:
25 Կահաթ	Կ	ՎՌԿԵ:
Ամրամ	Հ	ՎՁԼԵ:
Մովսէս	Ձ	ՎՊԺԵ:
Յանապատն	Խ	ՎՊԾԵ:
Յեսու նաւեայ	իԵ	ՎՊՂ:
30 Փենիէս	ՄԴ	ՎՁԴ:
Քուսարսաղ	Ը	ՎՁԺԱ:
Գողոնիէլ	Խ	ՎՁԾԱ:
Եգղոմ	ՃԸ	ՎՁԿԹ:
Աւովք եւ ամեկ	Ձ	Տխթ:
35 Աբիսացիբ	ի	Տկթ:
Դեբովրայ	Խ	Տծթ:
Ուրեք գեթ	Է	ՏծժՁ:
Գեդեոն	Խ	ՏծծՁ:
Աբիմելեք	Գ	Տծծթ:
40 Թովղայ	իԴ	Տծ2Բ:
Յայիր	իԲ	ՏՄԴ:
Ամոնացիբ	ՃԸ	ՏՄիԲ:
Յեփթայի	Զ	ՏՄիԸ:
Եսիրոն	Է	ՏՄԼԵ:
45 Աղղոնն	Ժ	ՏՄԽԵ:

	Jacob	85	2,55(2)
	Levi	46	(3,065)
25	Kohath	60	3,665
	Amram	70	3,735
	Moses	80	3,815
	In the desert	40	3,855
	Joshua b. Nun	25	3,880
30	Phineas	24	3,904
	(Cushan-Risha-thaim)	8	3,911
	Othniel	40	3,951
	Eglon	18	3,969
	Ehud and (Amalek)	80	4,049
35	Abisac'ik'	20	4,069
	Deborah	40	4,109
	Orēb, Zeeb	7	4,116
	Gideon	40	4,156
	Abimelech	3	4,159
40	Tola	24	4,182
	Jair	22	4,204
	Ammonites	18	4,222
	Jephtah	6	4,228
	Heshbon	7	4,235
45	Elon	10	4,245

	Արդոն	Լ	ՏՄԾԳ:
	Փոշտացիք	Խ	ՏՄՂԴ:
	Սամփսոն	ի	ՏՅԺԴ:
	Անիշխան	Խ	ՏՅԾԴ:
50	Հեդի	ի	ՏՅՀԴ:
	Սամուէլ	ի	ՏՅՂԴ:
	Սաւուղ	Խ	ՏՆԺԴ:
	Դաւիթ	Խ	ՏՆԾԴ:
	Սողոմոն	Խ	ՏՆՂԴ:
55	Րոբովամ	ԺԷ	ՏՃԺ:
	Աբդիու	Գ	ՏՃԺԴ:
	Ասափ	ԽՍ	ՏՃԾԵ:
	իյովասափաթ	իԵ	ՏՃՁՓ:
	Յովրամ	Լ	ՏՃՂԵ: /
211բ 60	Ոքոգիայ	Ս	ՏՃՂԼ:
	Գոթողիայ	Է	ՏՃՂԵ:
	Յովաս	Խ	ՏՈԼԵ:
	Ամասիայ .	իԹ	ՏՈԿԴ:
	Ոզիաս	ԾԲ	ՏՁԺՋ:
65	իյովաթամ	ԺՋ	ՏՋԼԲ:
	Աքազ	ԺՋ	ՏՋԽԲ:
	Եզեկիայ	իԹ	ՏՋՀԵ:
	Մանասէ	ԾԲ	ՏՊԼԲ:
	Ամովս	Բ	ՏՊԼԴ:

	Abdon	8	4,253
	Philistines	40	4,294
	Sampson	20	4,314
	No ruler	40	4,354
50	Eli	20	4,374
	Samuel	20	4,394
	Saul	40	4,414
	David	40	4,454
	Solomon	40	4,494
55	Rehoboam	17	4,51<1>
	(Abijah)	3	4,514
	(Asa)	41	4,555
	Jehosaphat	25	4,579
	Joram	8	4,587 /
211v			
60	Ahaziah	1	4,588
	Athaliah	7	4,595
	Joash	40	4,635
	Amaziah	29	4,664
	Uzziah	52	4,716
65	Jotham	16	4,732
	Ahaz	16	4,748
	Hezekiah	29	4,77<7>
	Manasseh	52	4,832
	(Amon)	2	4,834

70	Յովսիայ	ԼՍ	ՏՊԿԵ:
	Յովաբագ	Ս	ՏՊԿՋ:
	Եղիակիմ	ԺՍ	ՏՊՀԷ:
	Իյովակիմ	Ս	ՏՊՀԸ:
	Սեդեկիայ	ԺՍ	ՏՊՁԹ:
75	Նաբուգոթոնոսր	ԺՍ	ՏՋԺ:
	Նիրիկդիաթ	Ե	ՏՋԺԵ:
	Բադտասար	Գ	ՏՋԺԸ:
	Դարեհ Մար.	ԺԸ	ՏՋԼՋ:
	Կիւրոս	ԼԲ	ՏՋԿԸ:
80	Կամբիւսիս	Ը	ՏՋՀՋ:
	Յեսու առաջնորդ.	ԼԲ	ՐԸ:
	Իյովակիմ	Լ	ՐԼԸ:
	Եղիասիբոս	Խ	ՐՀԸ:
	Յովիդայէ	ԼՋ	ՐծԺԴ:
85	Իյովհաննէս	ԼԲ	ՐծԽՋ:
	Աբեդուս	Ի	ՐծԿՋ:
	Աւնինաս	ԻԲ	ՐծՋԸ:
	Սիմոն	ԺԵ	ՐՄԵ:
	Աւնիաս	ԺԴ	ՐՄԺԹ:
90	Եղիազար	ԼԲ	ՐՄծՍ:
	Մանասիս	ԻՋ	ՐՄՀԷ:

70	Josiah	31	4,865
	Jehoahaz	1	4,866
	Eliakim (Jehoiakim)	11	4,877
	Jehoiachin	1	4,878
	Zedekiah	11	4,889
75	Nebuchadnezzar	11	4,910
	Neriglissar	5	4,915
	Balthasar	3	4,918
	Darius the Mede	18	4,936
	Cyrus	32	4,968
80	Cambyses	8	4,976
	Joshua I	32	5,008
	Jehoiakim	30	5,038
	Eliashib	40	5,078
	Jehoiada	36	5,114
85	Johanan	32	5,146
	(Jaddua)	20	5,166
	Onias	22	5,188
	Simon	15	5,207
	Onias	14	5,219
90	Eleazar	32	5,251
	Manasseh	26	5,277

	Սիմոն	իԵ	ՐՅՔ:
	Իննիաս	Է	ՐՅիՁ:
	Իեսուս	Ձ	ՐՅԼՔ:
95	Իննիաս	Է	ՐՅԼԺ:
	Իննիաթէս.	ԺԵ	ՐՅՃՁ:
	Սիմոն	Ց	ՐՅԿԴ:
	Իյովաննէս	Լ	ՐՅՁԴ:
	Արիստաբուլլոս	Ա	ՐՅՁԵ:
100	Աղեքսանդրոս	Թ	ՐՆԴ:
	Յաննէոս	Լ	ՐՆԼԴ:
	Հիւրկիասոս	ԼԴ	ՐՆԿՑ:
	Հերովդէս	Դ	ՐՆՀՔ:
	Յուլիոս	Դ	ՐՆՀՁ:
105	Աւգոստոս	ԾՁ	ՐՇԼՔ:
	Տիբերիոս	իՔ	ՐՇՃԴ:
	Գայիոս	Դ	ՐՇՃՑ:
	Կղոդիոս	ԺԴ	ՐՇՀՔ:
	Ներոն	ԺԳ	ՐՇՁԵ:
110	Վէսպիանոս	Ժ	ՐՇՀԵ:
	Տիտոս	Գ	ՐՇՀՑ:
	Դոմետարիանոս	Ժ	ՐՈՑ:
	Տրայիանոս	ԺԹ	ՐՈիԵ:
	Անդրիանոս	իԱ	ՐՈԽՑ:

	Simon	25	5,302
	Onias	7	5,326
	Jesus	6	5,332
95	Onias	7	5,339
	Ioniat'ēs	17	5,356
	Simon	8	5,364
	Johanan	30	5,394
	Aristobulos	1	5,395
100	Alexander	9	5,404
	Jannaeus	30	5,434
	Hyrcanus	34	5,468
	Herod	4	5,472
	Julius	4	5,476
105	Augustus	56	5,532
	Tiberius	22	5,554
	Gaius	4	5,558
	Claudius	14	5,572
	Nero	13	5,585
110	Vespasian	10	5,595
	Titus	3	5,598
	Domitian	10	5,608
	Trajan	19	5,627
	Hadrian	21	5,648

115	Տիտոս	ԻԴ	ՐՈՀԲ:
	Մարկոս	(ԺԲ)	ՐՄՃ:
	Կոմոդոս	ԺԴ	ՐՃԵ:
	Սեւերոս	ԺԹ	ՐՃԻԴ:
	Անտոնինոս	Է	ՐՃԼԱ:
120	Միւս Անտոնինոս	Դ	ՐՃԼԵ:
	Ալեքսանդր	ԺԴ	ՐՃԽԹ: /
222ա	Մաքսիմիանոս	Գ	ՐՃԾԲ:
	Գորգիանոս	Ձ	ՐՃԾԸ:
	Փիլիպպոս	Ձ	ՐՃԿԴ:
125	Դեկոս	Բ	ՐՃԿՁ:
	Գալդոս	Գ	ՐՃԿԹ:
	Վալերիանոս	ԺԵ	ՐՁԲԴ:
	Գալիանոս	Բ	ՐՁԲԲ:
	Կլաւղէոս	Ա	ՐՁԲԷ:
130	Աւրեղիանոս	Ձ	ՐՁՂԴ:
	Աւրինտիդոս	Ա	ՐՁՂԴ:
	Պոռոս	Է	ՐՊԱ:
	Կարաոս	Բ	ՐՊԴ:
	Դիկոկղիտիանոս	ԺԲ	ՐՊԻ<Ե>:
135	Կոստանդիանոս	(ԺԲ)	ՐՊԼԷ:
	Նորին որդիքն	ԺԴ	ՐՊՂԱ:

115	Titus	24	5,672
	Marcus	⌈12⌉	5,691
	Commodus	14	5,705
	Severus	19	5,724
	Antoninus	7	5,731
120	Another Antoninus	4	5,735
	Alexander	14	5,749
	Maximinus	3	5,752
	(Gordian)	6	5,758
	Phillip	6	5,764
125	Decius	2	5,766
	(Gallus)	3	5,769
	Valerian	15	5,784
	Gallienus	2	5,786
	Claudius	1	5,787
130	Aurelian	6	5,793
	Awrindi̵los	1	5,794
	Probus	7	5,801
	Carus	2	5,803
	Diocletian	22	5,82(5)
135	Constantinus	⌈22⌉	5,857
	His son	24	5,881

Յուլիանոս	Ա	ՐՂՁԲ:
Վաղէնտիոս	Է	ՐՂՁԹ:
Վաղէս	Ձ	ՐՂՂԵ:
140 Գրատիանոս	Ձ	ՐՂՃԱ:
Թէոթոս մեծ	ԺԵ	ՐՂՃՂ:
Նորին որդիքն	ԻԴ	ՐՂԽ:
Թէոդոս փոքր	ԼԷ	ՐՂՀԷ:
Մարկիանոս	Է	ՐՂՁԴ:
145 Զենունդեանք	ԺԹ	ՑԴ:
Զենոն	ԺԲ	ՑԻԱ:
Անաստաս	(ԻԷ)	ՑԽԲ:
Յուստինիանոս	Թ	ՑԵԷ:
Իուստինոս	ԼԲ	ՑՀԵ:
150 Իուստինոս	ԺԱ	ՑՁՂ:
Տիբերեոս	Ձ	ՑՁՁԲ:
Մորիկոս	Ի	ՑՁԼԲ:
Փաւկաս	Բ	ՑՁԽ:
Երակլիոս	Լ	ՑՁՀ:
155 Կոստանդինոս	Ա	ՑՁՀ(Գ):
Կոստանդին	Բ	ՑՁՀԳ:

Լինին յԱդամայ մինչեւ ցայս վայր ամբ ՑՁՀԳ:

	Julian	1	5,882
	Valentinian	7	5,889
	Valens	6	5,895
140	Gratian	6	5,901
	Theodosius the Great	15	5,916
	His sons	24	5,940
	Theodosius The Less	37	5,977
	Marcian	7	5,984
145	The Leos	19	6,003
	Zeno	18	6,021
	Anastasius	⌈25⌉	6,048
	Justinian	9	6,057
	Justin	38	6,095
150	Justin	11	6,106
	Tiberius	6	6,112
	Maurice	20	6,132
	Phocas	8	6,140
	Heraclius	30	6,170
155	Constantinus	1	6,17⌈3⌉
	Constans	2	6,173

These are 6,173 years from Adam up to this place.

ln 5   Arm has, literally Malaliel, a corrupted form
        of this name.

ln 7   MS has 1,295 for 1,297 arising from graphic
        error ḅ for ẓ .

ln 13   Kainan: So LXX Gen 11:13, Luke 3:36.

ln 15   The reading for the name is unclear in the MS.

ln 17   MS has omitted final numeral, 7. There are two
        difficulties in the figures: If the total for
        Peleg is amended to 2,895, then between Peleg
        and Nahor there should have elapsed, by the
        totals, 241 years, but 132 + 130 + 79 produces
        341. Apparently an extra hundred years have
        entered at this point.

ln 20   For Isaac the totals imply a span of 166, opposed
        to the 60 offered.

ln 22   The total for Jacob implies a span of 80 or,
        alternatively the total should read 3,557.

ln 23   The total for Levi is corrupt and irretrievable
        on textual grounds. Extrapolating back from the
        coherent totals for Kohath and Amram, the total
        should be 3,605, but then the length of span for
        Levi should be the difference between 3,605 and
        either 3,552 or 3,557, i.e. 48 or 53.

ln 30   Addition off by one number.

ln 31   See Jud 3:7-11. Armenian reads a somewhat
        corrupt "K'usarsad".

ln 34   The MS reads "Awovk' and Amek". The first name
        is recognizably corrupt for the Armenian of
        "Ehud". The second is perhaps to be read as
        suggested here, cf. Jud 3:13.

ln 35   Abišu – the name apparently resembles Abishua
        the Levite, Phineas' son (1 Chr 6:4) – who was
        high priest after Phineas, so The Chronicle, p.
        50 citing older sources. It is not, however,
        probable that a high priest is referred to here,
        and perhaps the name is related to "Jabin and
        Sisera".

ln 37   The second name is corrupted to "Zēt'" in the
        MS.

ln 40   The total for this line is off by one.

ln 47   Total corrupt, inner-Armenian for 4,293 or one
        year short in span.

ln 55   Apparently the number "1" has been lost follow-
        ing this total.

ln 56   The text reads "Abdiu", i.e. Obadiah, a corrup-
        tion, cf. 1 Kings 15:2

ln 57   MS gives corrupt "Asaph".

ln 58   The span appears to be one off.

ln 62   The MS reads "Yozas".

ln 67   The totals or the spans for this plus the follow-
        ing lines are off: 4,758 + 29 = 4,777 (not
        4,755) + 52 = 4,829 (or 4,827) not 4,832, which
        implies a span of 55 or 57.

ln 69   MS reads "Amos".

ln 75   The totals are off, 4,889 + 11 = 4,900 not 4,911.

ln 76   Apparently Neriglissar is referred to by this
        entry, which in the MS reads "Nirigłiat".

ln 86   The MS reads "Abedus".

ln 87   The MS reads "Awninas", cf. Jos. <u>Ant</u>. 5.2.7.

ln 89   The span of "14" is apparently corrupt for
             "12" - graphic.

ln 93   The span "7" is apparently corrupt for "24",
             perhaps by dittography from ln 95.

ln 96   Alcimus would be expected here. The name is
             not readily to be identified, but it may be
             corruption of "Jonathan". The order of events
             in the following lines is confused.

ln 100   Text reads "Hiwrkiasos".

ln 112   "Dometrianos" in the manuscript.

ln 114   "A n drianos" in the manuscript. Nerva is
             omitted, preceding Trajan.

ln 115   "Titus" is apparently corrupt for "Antonius
             Pius", perhaps by some sort of dittography
             from ln 111, <u>supra</u>.

ln 116   "12" is apparently corrupt for "19" by the not
             uncommon graphic confusion of ϱ and θ.

ln 119   i.e. Caracalla, officially named M. Aurelius
             Antoninus.

ln 120   i.e. Elagabalus, who took the name M.Aurelius
              Antoninus

ln 123   MS has corrupt "Gorgian" by graphic error ϱ/η.

ln 126   The MS has "Galdus" by graphic error η/η.

ln 131   This is apparently a corruption of some name,
             perhaps Florianus, but is not clear.

ln 134   The MS has 5,827, by graphic error b/ζ.

ln 135   The span " 22" is apparently corrupt for "32"
             by dittography.

ln 139   The MS reads "Va‡ēs"

ln 145   The span of 25 is corrupt for 28 by graphic
            error ℎ/ꞓ.

ln 148-149 The order of the names of Justin and Justin-
            ian should be reversed.

ln 155   The total is corrupt for 6,171.

NOTES

1 Ճամանակագրութիւն Տեառն Միքայէլի Ասորւոց Պատրիարքի
(The Chronicle of Lord Michael, Patriarch of the Syrians;
Jerusalem: St. James, 1871).

2 Cited according to J.-B. Chabot, Chronique de Michel le
Syrien (repr. Bruxelles: Culture et Civilisation, 1963)
15-17.

3 Cited according to C. Bezold, Die Schatzhöhle (Leip-
zig: Hinrichs, 1883-86). Bezold offers a Syriac text
and a German translation.

4 C.J.F. Dowsett(ed. and tr.) The History of the Caucas-
sian Albanians by Movses Dasxuranc'i (London: O.U.P.,
1961) 1-2.

5 B. Sarghissian, Անանուն Ճամանկագրութիւն (Anonymous
Chronicle; Venice: Mechitarists, 1904); the fullest
discussion is in the study by Markwart included in the
second edition of A. Bauer's edition of Hippolytus'
Chronicle (GCS 46; Berlin: Helm, 1955) 142-143.

6 Op., cit., p. xxv.

INDEX TO ONOMASTICA

Numbers refer to Onomasticon, Sample and line in that order.

Ա̅բ̅աբ̅ովթ̅	Ababovt'	I v A 30, 40, C 34, E 1a, F 18
Աբանայ	Abana	I v A 33, C 33, E 1, F 17
Աբարիմ	Abarim (s.v.)	III 2, V 3
Աբբա	Abba	I v A 31, C 32, D 1, E 2, F 13, III 1, IV 27, V 2
Աբբաէղ	Abbaēł	I v A 34, C 33, D 4, E 4, F 16
Աբբանա	Abbana (s.v.)	I v A 29, C 31, D 2, E 3, F 15, VI i 1
Աբբեթդարա	Abbet'dara	I v D 10
Աբբէղ	Abbēł	I v E 4a
Աբբիայ	Abbia	I v A 26, C 30, 32, E 5, F 14
Աբբոկ	Abbok	I v D 6
Աբբոր	Abbor	I v D 3, VI i 2
Աբդենագո	Abdenagō	III 4, V 8
Աբդիաս	Abdias	See Աբդիւ Abdiu
Աբդիմելէք	Abdimelēk' (s.v.) III 3, V 5, 16 app.	
Աբդիւ	Abdiu	I v A 27, C 38, D 8, E 6, F 19 III 5, v 4
Աբդլմսեհ	Abdlmseh	I v D 7, VI i 3
Աբդոն	Abdōn (s.v.)	III 6, V 6
Աբեդդար	Abeddar	I v C 19, E 7, F 23, V 7
Աբեդնագով	Abednagov	See Աբդենագո Abdenago
Աբել	Abel	I iv 2, v A 14, 34, B 2, C 14 D 13, E 9, F 25, III 7, 8, IV 2, V 9, 10
Աբեղ	Abeł	See Աբել Abel
Աբեղա	Abeła	I v A 38, C 16, D 9, E 8, F 24, VI i 4
Աբեղբի	Abełbi (s.v.)	I v A 36, C 20, D 11, E 10, F 27

Աբեղմայուդայ Abełmayuła (s.v.) I v A 25, C 15, D 14, E 11
                                    F 22
Աբենեզեր   Abenēzer   I v A 23, B 48, C 18, D 12,
                                    E 12, F 21
Աբեննէր   Abennēr (s.v.)   I v A 22, B 45, C 17, D 5,
                                    E 13, F 20, III 18, V 11
Աբեսողոմ   Abēsołom (s.v.)   I v A 21, B 42, C 28, D 20,
                                    E 14, F 26, III 9, IV 12,
                                    V 12

Աբիա   Abia   I v D 21, E 16, III 10,
                                    V 13
Աբիաթար   Abiat'ar   I v A 20, B 37, C 26, D 18,
                                    E 15, F 28, III 11, V 14
Աբիան   Abian   VI i 5

Աբիգալ   Abigal   III 13 app.

Աբիգայ   Abiga   III 13

Աբիգայիլ   Abigayil   III 12, V 15 comm.

Աբիգան   Abigan   I iv 20 app.

Աբիգեայ   Abigea (s.v.)   I v A 19, B 39, C 27, F 29
Աբիդա   Abida   I v D 19
Աբիդան   Abidan (s.v.)   I iv 20, v A 18, B 18,
                                    C 25, D 17, E 18, F 30
Աբիդաս   Abidas   III 5 app

Աբիդար   Abidar   I v B 19, D 18

Աբիդդար   Abiddar   I v A 24

Աբիդեա   Abidea   I v E 17

Աբիեսսեա   Abiessea   V 18

Աբիմեղեք   Abimełek' (s.v.)   I iv 11, v A 17, B 11, 13,
                                    C 24, D 16, E 19, F 31,
                                    III 14, IV 5, V 16, 79 app.

Աբինադաբ   Abinadab   III 15, V 17

Աբիոն   Abion   I v A 28, C 35, D 15, E 20,
                                    F 32
Աբիուդ   Abiud   I v A 37, C 37, D 23, E 21,
                                    F 33
Աբիուրիմ   Abiurim   I v A 35, C 36, D 22, E 22,
                                    F 34
Աբիսակ   Abisak   I v A 30, C 29, E 23, F 35,
                                    III 16, V 19
Աբներ   Abner   III 17   See Աբեննէր
                                                Abennēr

Աբոտ	Abot (s.v.)	I v C 39, D 24, E 24, F 36
Աբրաթ	Abrat'	I v A 32, D 28, E 26
Աբրահամ	Abraham (s.v.)	I iv 7, v A 15, 16, B 7, C 22, D 27, E 25, F 38, IV 45, V 21
Աբրայ	Abra (s.v.)	I v D 25, F 40, III 19, V 20, VI i 6
Աբրամ	Abram	I iv 6, v A 15, B 6, C 21, D 26, E 27, F 37, III 20, V 21 app., 22
Աբրոկ	Abrok	I v A 41, C 23, E 27a
Աբրոտ	Abrot	I v A 39
Ագաբ	Agab	V 23
Ագաբոս	Agabos (s.v.)	I v A 43, C 41, D 38, E 28, F 43, V 23 app.
Ագաբրամթովն	Agabŕamt'ovn	I v E 30
Ագագ	Agag	I iv 17, v A 41, 44, C 43, D 35, E 29, V 24, VI i 14.
Ագադ	Agad	I iv 17 app.
Ագաթանգեղոս	Agat'angełōs	I v D 31, VI i 10
Ագաթռեմովթ	Agat'ŕemovt' (s.v.)	I v D 33, VI i 11
Ագահ	Agah	V 23 app, VI i 9
Ագան	Agan	V 25
ագանել		I v D 34, VI i 13
Ագանովթայ	Aganovt'a	VI i 16
Ագապ	Agap	I v D 30, VI i 8
Ագապէն	Agapēn	I v D 29, VI i 7
ագասութիւն		I v D 36, VI i 15
Ագար	Agar	I iv 8, v A 40, B 8, C 40, E 31, F 41, V 26
ագարակ		VI i 12
ագարակբ		I v D 32
Ագարսա	Agarsa	I v D 37
Ագբակ	Agbak	IV 31

Ադոնիբեզեկ	Adonibezek	I iv 30, v A 4, B 24, C 7, E 40, F 3
Ադոնիզեբեկ	Adonizebek	See Ադոնիբեզեկ Adonibezek
Ադոնիէլ	Adoniēl	I v A 11, C 10, E 43, F 6
Ադոնիրամ	Adoniram	I v F 4
Ադոնմոյ	Adonmo	VI i 32
Ադովնայ	Adovna (s.v.)	I v A 8, C 8, E 41, F 5, IV 20, V 28, VI i 27
Ադովնիայ	Adovnia	I v A 9, C 9, E 42, F 7, IV 21, V 29 app., 30
Ադրաազար	Adraazar (s.v.)	I v A 6, C 12, E 44, F 12
Ադրամեղեք	Adrameɫek' (s.v.)	I v A 7, C 13, E 45, F 11, VI i 31 app.
Ազազայէլ	Azazayēl	I V E 46, F 47
Ազազիէլ	Azaziēl	IV 17
ազագուն		VI i 33
Ազայէլ	Azayēl	I v E 47, F 46
Ազան	Azan	I iv 31, v B 25, E 48, F 45
Ազապարայ	Azabara	I v E 49
Ազար	Azar	I v E 50, F 48
Ազարիայ	Azaria	I v F 49, IV 23, V 31,
ազգ		VI i 34
ազդեր		VI i 37
Ազդէովթ	Azdēovt'	VI i 38
ազդր		VI i 36
ազղող		VI i 35
Ազեկայ	Azeka	VI i 39
Ազմոլդեւ	Azmoldew	VI i 40
Ազոտոս	Azotos (s.v.)	I iv 37, v B 31, V 32
Ազդվր	Azdvr	V 33
Աթաղիա	At'aɫia	V 34

Ալելուիա	Aleluia (s.v.)	I v B 50, IV 15, V 38
Ալեփ	Alep'	I ii 1
Ակիտաբէլ	Akitabēl	See Ak'itop'el
Ակկարոն	Akkaron	I iv 39, v B 33, V 35
Ակրաբիմ	Akrabim	I iv 32, v B 26
Աֆարովն	Aharovn (s.v.)	I iv 19, v B 17, IV 7, V 36
Աֆովտ	Ahovt	V 37
Աղեկսանդէր	Aɫeksandēr	V 39
Աղեկսանդրիայ	Aɫeksandria	V 40
Ամաղեք	Amaɫek' (s.v.)	I iv 29, v B 23, IV 9, V 41
Ամամ	Amam	V 42
Աման	Aman	V 43
Ամանայ	Amana	V 44
Ամասիայ	Amasia	IV 30, V 47
Ամատտարա	Amattara	I v B 38
Ամարփաղ	Amarp'aɫ	I iv 10, v B 10
Ամբակում	Ambakum	IV 28, V 45
Ամեսսայի	Amessai (s.v.)	I v B 47, V 47 app., 48
Ամէն	Amēn	IV 26, V 49
Ամէսիա	Amēsia	V 48 app.
Ամինադաբ	Aminadab	I iv 16, v B 15, IV 6, V 50
Ամմովն	Ammovn	I iv 12, v B 12, V 51
Ամնոն	Amnon	I iv 12 app., v 11, V 52, comm.
Ամոն	Amon	V 51 app., 52
Ամովս	Amovs	V 53, 54
Ամովսիայ	Amovsia	IV 16
Ամուրֆացի	Amurhac'i	I iv 28, v B 22, IV· 8, V 55

Ամրամ	Amram	I iv 18, v B 16
Ամրի	Amri	v 46
Այենդովր	Ayendovr	I v B 41
Անաբովթ	Anabovt	See Անաթովթ Anat'ovt'
Անաթովթ	Anat'ovt'	I iv 33, v B 27, IV 10, V 57
Անանիայ	Anania	IV 22, V 56
Անգէաս	Angēas	V 58
Անգէ	Angē	V 58 comm.
անդրադարձումն		IV 41
Անդրիաս	Andrias (s.v.)	IV 25, V 59
անրնդհատ		IV 37
Անթրակ	Ant'rak	I iv 25
Աննա	Anna	I iv 36, v B 30, IV 11, V 60
անուրջ		IV 36
անշրպետ		IV 38
Անտիոքիա	Antiok'ia	V 61
Անքուս	Ank'us	I v B 40
ապաշաւիլ		IV 40
Ապողոս	Apołos	V 62
Առած	Ařac	I iv 23, IV 29
առհաւատչեա		IV 39
Ասաել	Asael	I v B 46
Ասաթ	Asat'	I iv 15
Ասափ	Asap'	I v B 49
Ասեր	Aser	I iv 13, v B 13, V 63
Ասերովթ	Aserovt'	I iv 27 app., v B 19
Ասերովն	Aserovn	I iv 26 app., 27, v B 21

Ասթինէ	Ast'inē	V 64
Ասկալովն	Askalovn	I iv 38, v B 32, 33
Ասուր	Asur	I iv 5, v B 5, IV 19, V 65
Ասվերուս	Asverus	V 66
Աստարովթ	Astarovt'	V 67
Աստին	Astin	I v B 50
Ասրովն	Asrovn	I iv 22
Ասքա	Ask'a	V 68
Արա	Ara	I v C 49
Արաբացիք	Arabac'ik'	V 69, 70
Արաբիա	Arabia	I v C 48
Արաբովթ	Arabovt'	I v A 45, C 45
Արամ	Aram	I iv 14, 18 app., v A 46, B 141, C 46, V 71
Արամաթի	Aramat'i	I v C 47
Արարատ	Ararat	V 72, 260
Արբոկ	Arbok	V 73
արգասաւոր		IV 33
արգաւանդ		IV 32
արդարել		IV 34
Արիմաթեմ	Arimat'em (s.v.)	I iv 40, v A 48, B 34, IV 13
Արիոպագոս	Ariopagos	V 74
Արիովն	Ariovn	I iv 26
Արիսպագոս	Arispagos	I v A 50
Արոն	Aron	I iv 22 app., V 75
արուարձան		IV 35
Արուէլ	Aruēl	I iv 34 app., v A 47, B 28
Արուէր	Aruēr	I iv 34, v B 28

Արտաքսերքսէս	Artak'serk'se̅s	V 76
Արրա	Arra	I v C 50
Արփաքսաթ	Arp'ak'sat'	I iv 4, v A 44, B 4, C 44, IV 3, V 77
Արքեղաւոս	Ark'eławos	I v A 49
Աւգոստոս	Awgo̅stos	IV 24
Աւնան	Awnan	I iv 9, v B 9
Աւովդ	Awovd (s.v.)	I iv 35, v B 29
Ափփուսովթ	Ap'p'usovt'	I iv 24
Աքազ	Ak'az	IV 18, V 81
Աքայիա	Ak'ayia	V 80
Աքայեաբ	Akayeab	V 78
Աքարիմ	Ʌk'arim	I iv 21 app.
Աքերովք	Ak'erovk'	I v B 35
Աքիմաաս	Ak'imaas	I v B 44
Աքիմելեք	Ak'imelek'	I v B 36, V 79
Աքիտոփել	Ak'itop'el	I v B 43, IV 14, V 82
Աքիրամ	Ak'iram	I iv 21, v B 20
Աքուս	Ak'us	See Ank'us
Բաալ	Baal	VI ii 3
Բաաղ	Baał	VI ii 4
Բաաղիմ	Baałim	VI ii 5
Բաբայ	Baba	VI ii 1
Բաբելոն	Babelon	IV 42, VI ii 6
Բաբէլ	Babe̅l	V 83
Բաէլ	Bae̅l	VI ii 2
Բաթուէ	Bat'ue̅	V 84

Բենիամին	Beniamin	IV 43, V 116
Բենոնի	Benoni	V 117
Բեսելիէլ	Beseliēl	IV 48
Բետուլ	Betul	V 118
Բերա	Bera	V 119
Բերովբա	Berovba	IV 56
Բերսաբէ	Bersabē	IV 49, V 107, 110
Բէլ	Bēl	IV 45, V 122
Բէրեսիթ	Bērēsit'	V 126 app.
Բոյոս	Boyos	V 124
Բոսոր	Bosor	IV 47, V 125
Բրեսիթ	Bresit'	V 126
Գաբայա	Gabaya	V 127 app.
Գաբայադ	Gabayad	V 128
Գաբայեա	Gabayea	V 127
Գաբրիէլ	Gabriēl	V 129
Գադգադ	Gadgad	V 131
Գազեր	Gazer	V 132
Գաթ	Gat'	V 130
Գալաադ	Galaad	V 245 comm.
Գալիլեա	Galilea	V 133
Գալատացիք	Galatac'ik'	V 134
Գաղգաղայ	Gałgałay	V 135
Գաղգոթայ	Gałgot'a	V 143
Գեբաղ	Gebał	V 136
Գեդէոն	Gedēon	V 137
Գեհենին	Gehenin	V 139
Գեհոն	Gehon	V 138
Գերսոմ	Gersom	V 140
Գերսոն	Gerson	V 141
Գէթոն	Gēt'on	V 137 app.
Գոգ	Gog	V 142
Գոլմոր	Golmor	V 145 app.
Գողիաթ	Gołiat'	V 144
Գոմեր	Gomer	V 145
Գոմորայ	Gomora	V 146

Դաբրէիմովմին	Dabrēiovmin	V 147
Դագան	Dagan	V 148
Դաթան	Dat'an	V 150
Դալիա	Dalia	V 149 app.
Դալիլա	Dalila	V 149
Դաղեթ	Dałet'	I ii 4
Դամասկոս	Damaskus	V 151
Դան	Dan	V 152
Դանիէլ	Daniēl	V 153
Դարեհ	Dareh	V 154
Դաւիթ	Dawit'	V 155
Դեբովրա	Debovra	V 156
Դիկապոլիս	Dekapōlis	V 157
Դիաբոլոս	Diabolos	V 158
Դիապոլոս	Diapolos	V 158 app.
Դիդիմոս	Didimos	V 159
Դիթալասոն	Dit'alason	V 160
Դինա	Dina	V 161
Դիոնիսիոս	Dionisios	V 162
Դովեկ	Dovek	V 163
Դովր	Dovr	V 164
Դովրա	Dovra	V 165
Եբաղ	Ebał	V 166
Եբեր	Eber	V 167
Եբրայեցի	Ebrayec'i	V 168
Եգիպտոս	Egiptos	V 169
Եգղոմ	Egłom	V 170
Եդեմ	Edem	V 171
Եդոմ	Edom	V 172
Եզեկիա	Ezekia	V 173
Եզեկիէլ	Ezekiēl	V 174
Եզրաս	Ezras	V 175
Եզրիէլ	Ezriēl	V 176
Եզրով	Ezrov	V 177
Եթամ	Et'am	V 178
Եթովպիա	Et'ovpia	V 179

Ելգանայ	Elgana	V 180
Ելեքանան	Elek'anan	V 181 app.
Ելքանան	Elk'anan	V 181
Եկլեսիաստէս	Eklesiastēs	V 189
Եղիա	Ełia	V 182
Եղիազար	Ełiazar	V 184
Եղիակիմ	Ełiakim	V 183
Եղիմելէք	Ełimelēk'	V 185
Եղինաթան	Ełinat'an	V 186
Եղիշէ	Ełišē	V 187
Եղիսաբեթ	Ełisabet'	V 188
Եմաւուս	Emawus	V 190
Եմմանուէլ	Emmanuēl	V 191
Եյ	Ey	See Ec'
Ենգենիա	Engenia	V 192
Եննոն	Ennon	V 193
Ենովս	Enovs	V 194
Ենովք	Enovk'	V 195
Եսայիայ	Esayia	V 196
Եսաւ	Esaw	V 197
Եսթեր	Est'er	V 198
Երեմէէլ	Eremēēl	V 200
Երեմիա	Eremia	V 201
Երիքով	Erik'ov	V 202
Երուսաղէմ	Erusałem	V 203
Եւա	Ewa	V 204
Եւբուլոս	Ewbulos	V 199
Եփրաթայ	Ep'rat'a	V 205
Եփրայիմ	Ep'rayim	V 206
Եփրոն	Ep'ron	V 207
Եց	Ec'	I ii 16
Զաբոն	Zabon	V 208 app.
Զաբուղուն	Zabułun	V 208
Զամրի	Zamri	V 209
Զարայ	Zara	V 210
Զաքարիայ	Zak'aria	V 211

Զաքէոս	Zak'ēos	V 212
Զեբեդեա	Zebedea	V 213
Զեբէէ	Zebēē	V 214
Զէ	Zē	I ii 7
Զլլէսմովդ	Zllēsmovd	V 216 app.
Զորաբաբէլ	Zōrababēl	V 215
Էլլէսմովթ	Ēllēsmovt'	V 216
Թադէոս	T'adēos	V 217
Թամար	T'amar	V 218
Թարայ	T'ara	V 219
Թարսիս	T'arsis	V 220
Թաւ	T'aw	I ii 22, V 221
Թափոր	T'ap'or	V 222
Թերաթիմ	T'erat'im	V 223
Թոբէլ	T'obel	V 224
Թով	T'ov	V 225 app.
Թովմաս	T'ovmas	V 225
Թոփոթոր	T'op'ot'or	V 226
Իեզրայէլ	Iezrayēl	V 227
Իթամար	It'amar	V 228
Իսահակ	Isahak	V 229
Իսաքար	Isak'ar	V 230
Իսմայէլ	Ismayēl	V 231
Իսրայէլ	Israyēl	V 232
Լիա	Lia	V 233
Լիբանոս	Libanos	V 234
Լիբիա	Libia	V 235
Լիթոստրատոս	Lit'ostratos	V 236
Խաթէս	Xat'ēs	V 238 app.
Խառան	Xaran	V 237
Խեթ	Xet'	I ii 8
Ծադէ	Cadē	I ii 18
Կադէս	Kadēs	V 238
Կազդին	Kazdin	V 485
Կահաթ	Kahat'	V 239
Կային	Kayin	V 240

Կանա	Kana	V 241
Կասթին	Kast'in	v 242
Կարիաթարիմ	Kariat'arim	V 243
Կարիաթսեփեր	Kariat'sep'ēr	V 244
կարկառ		V 245
Կարմէլ	Karmēl	V 246
Կափառնայում	Kap'arnayum	V 247
Կեդար	Kedar	V 248
Կեդրոն	Kedron	V 249
Կերէաս	Kerēas	V 250
Կեփաս	Kep'as	V 251
Կինովթ	Kinovt'	V 252
Կիպրոս	Kipros	V 255
Կիս	Kis	V 253
Կիւրոս	Kiwros	V 256
Կղէոպաս	Kłēopas	V 254
Կողոսացիք	Kołosac'ik'	V 257
Կորբան	Korban	V 258
Կորխա	Korxa	V 259
Կոփ	Kop'	I ii 19
Հաբէղ	Habeł	III 7 app, See Abeł
Հայաստան	Hayastan	V 260
Հելի	Heli	V 262
Հելիպաօղիս	Helipołis	V 263
Հերմոն	Hermon	V 261
Հէ	Hē	I ii 5
Հնդիկք	Hndikk'	V 265
Հնդաստան	Hndstan	V 264
Հոլեփեռնէս	Hołep'ernēs	V 266
Հռոմ	Hrom	V 267
Հռութ	Hrut'	V 268
Ղաբան	Łaban	V 269
Ղազարոս	Łazaros	V 270
Ղամեդ	Łamed	I ii 12
Ղամէք	Lamēk'	V 271
Ղապիովթ	Łapiovt'	V 272

Ղեկի	Łeki	V 273
Ղեւի	Łewi	V 274
Ղեւիաթան	Łewiat'an	V 276
Ղեքի	Łek'i	V 275
Ղովտ	Łovt	V 277
Մաաքեա	Maak'ea	V 279
Մագդաղենացի	Magdałenac'i	V 282
Մադիան	Madian	V 280
Մաթէոս	Mat'ēos	V 296
Մաթուսաղայ	Mat'usała	V 281
Մակեդոն	Makedon	V 283
Մաղաքիայ	Małak'ia	V 284
Մաղեղէթ	Małelēt'	V 285
Մաղքոս	Małk'os	V 286
Մամզէր	Mamzēr	V 287
Մամոնայ	Mamona	V 288
Մայասիա	Mayasia	V 278
Մանայեմ	Manayem	V 289
Մանասէ	Manasē	V 290
Մանովէ	Manovē	V 291
Մառա	Mařa	V 292
Մասաղոթ	Masałot'	V 293
Մասեփտ	Masep't	V 294
Մասսա	Massa	V 295
Մարթայ	Mart'ay	V 297
Մարիամ	Mariam	V 298
Մելքիա	Melk'ia	V 299
Մելքիսեդեկ	Melk'isedek	V 300
Մելքիսուայ	Melk'isua	V 301
Մելքող	Melk'oł	V 302
Մեղքայ	Mełkay	V 307
Մեմ	Mēm	I ii 13
Մեմփիբոստէ	Memp'ibostē	V 303
Մեսողամ	Mesołam	V 304
Մեսոպոտանիա	Mesopotania	V 305
Միսափաթ	Misap'at'	V 306

Միսայէլ	Misayēl	V 312
Միսիա	Misia	V 310
Միքա	Mik'a	V 308
Միքայէլ	Mik'ayēl	V 309
Միքիա	Mik'ia	V 311
Մնէս	Mnēs	V 313
Մոգ	Moç	V 317
Մովաբ	Movab	V 314
Մովաս	Movas	V 315 app.
Մովսա	Movsa	V 315
Մովսէս	Movsēs	V 316
Յաբէթ	Yabet'	V 323
Յակոբ	Yakob	V 318
Յամին	Yamin	V 319
Յայէլ	Yayēl	V 320
Յայիէլ	Yayiēl	V 321
Յասոն	Yason	V 322
Յեբուս	Yebus	V 324
Յեբուսթէ	Yebust'ē	V 326
Յեդովմէ	Yedovmē	V 355
Յեզոնիա	Yezonia	V 356
Յեմենի	Yemeni	V 327
Յեսբոք	Yesbōk	V 330
Յեսու	Yesu	V 332
Յեսսէ	Yessē	V 331
Յերապոլիս	Yerapōlis	V 325
Յերոբոադ	Yeroboał	V 333
Յերոբովամ	Yerobovam	V 334
Յեւայիմ	Yewayim	V 360
Յեփթայէ	Yep't'ayē	V 335
Յեքոնիա	Yek'onia	V 338
Յէու	Yēu	V 328
Յէուս	Yēus	V 329
Յիսուս	Yisus	V 336
Յոբ	Yob	V 339
Յոթորայ	Yot'ora	V 337

Յոյնք	Yoynk'	V 360
Յովաբ	Yovab	V 343
Յովակիմ	Yovakim	V 344
Յովաս	Yovas	V 345
Յովաքիմ	Yovak'im	V 346
Յովդ	Yovd	See C'ovd
Յովէլ	Yovel	V 347
Յովհաննէս	Yovhannēs	V 348
Յովնադաբ	Yovnadab	V 349
Յովնաթան	Yovnat'an	V 350
Յովնան	Yovnan	V 351
Յովսափատ	Yovsap'at	V 352
Յովսէփ	Yovsēp'	V 353
Յովսիա	Yovsia	V 354
Յովրամ	Yovram	V 357
Յորդանան	Yordanan	V 358
Յուդայ	Yuda	V 340
Յուլիոս	Yulios	V 341
Յունան	Yunan	V 342
Յոքազ	Yok'az	V 359 app.
Յոքաս	Yok'as	V 359
Նաբաթ	Nabat'	V 362, 383 app.
Նաբաղ	Nabał	V 363
Նաբովթ	Nabovt'	V 364
Նաբուգոդոնոսոր	Nabugodonosor	V 365
Նազարեթ	Nazaret'	V 366
Նազովրացիք	Nazovrac'ik'	V 367
Նաթան	Nat'an	V 368
Նաթանայէլ	Nat'anayēl	V 369
Նայասոն	Nayason	V 361
Նային	Nayin	V 369 app., 370
Նանթան	Nant'an	V 368 app.
Նաւում	Nawum	V 371
Նաքովր	Nak'ovr	V 372
Նեբրովթ	Nebrovt'	V 375
Նեփթայիմ	Nep't'ayim	V 378

Ն էապօլիս	Nēapōlis	V 374
Ն է եման	Nēeman	V 373
Ն է եմի	Nēemi	V 376
Ն է ովստան	Nēovstan	V 377
Ն ինուէ	Ninuc̄	V 379
Ն ոյ	Noy	V 380
Ն ոյոմին	Noyomin	V 381
Ն ու արեղղաբր	Nuareddabr	V 383
Ն ուն	Nun	I ii 14
Շ աբաթ	Šabat'	V 383
Շ ին	Šin	I ii 21
Շ ուշանայ	Šušana	V 384
Ո ղողոմ	Odołom	V 385
Ո զա	Oza	V 387
Ո զիա	Ozia	V 388
Ո զիէ լ	Oziēl	V 389
Ո ղա	Oła	V 390
Ո ղբաղիայ	Ołbadia	V 392 app.
Ո ն է սիմէ ոս	Onēsimēos	V 386
Ո ռնան	Ołnan	V 391
Ո վբաթիա	Ovbat'ia	V 392
Ո վբէ թ	Ovbēt'	V 393
Ո վնանայ	Ovnana	V 395
Ո վսէ է	Ovsēē	V 396
Ո վրէ փ	Ovrēp'	V 397
Ո վք	Ovk'	V 394
Ո րղիեկրայ	Ordiekra	V 398
Ո ւ լա	Ula	V 387 app.
Ո ւրիա	Uria	V 399
Ո քոզիա	Ok'ozia	V 400
Պ աղիստինէ	Pałistinē	V 401
Պ ասեք	Pasek'	V 403
Պ արասկեւէ	Paraskewē	V 402
Պ ենտէ կոստ	Pentēkost	V 404
Պ եարոս	Petros	V 405
Ջ երոնիմոս	Jeronimos	V 406

Ռաբաթ	Ṙabat'	V 407
Ռագուէլ	Ṙaguēl	V 408
Ռախաբ	Ṙaxab	V 409
Ռահաբ	Ṙahab	V 410
Ռամայ	Ṙama	V 411
Ռամեսէ	Ṙamesē	V 412
Ռափայէլ	Ṙap'ayēl	V 413
Ռափայիմ	Ṙap'ayim	V 414
Ռաքէլ	Ṙak'el	V 415
Ռեբեկայ	Ṙebeka	V 418
Ռեմոն	Ṙemon	V 416
Ռեսփայ	Ṙesp'ay	V 417
Ռեփա	Ṙep'a	V 417 app.
Ռեքաբ	Ṙek'ab	V 419
Ռուբէն	Ṙubēn	V 420
Ռոբովամ	Ṙobovam	V 421
Սաբայ	Saba	V 422
Սաբաովթ	Sabaovt	V 423
Սադուկեցիք	Sadukec'ik'	V 424
Սաղա	Saɫa	V 425
Սաղիմ	Saɫim	V 426
Սաղմանասար	Saɫmanasar	V 427
Սաղմոն	Saɫmon	V 428
Սաղպաաղ	Saɫpaad	V 429
Սամարիա	Samaria	V 430
Սամուէլ	Samuēl	V 432
Սամքաթ	Samk'at'	I ii 15
Սամփսոն	Samp'son	V 431
Սառայ	Saṙa (s.v.)	V 422 app., 433
Սատանայ	Satana	V 434
Սարայի	Sarayi	V 435
Սարոնայ	Sarona	V 436
Սաւուղ	Sawuɫ	V 437
Սափատ	Sap'at	V 438
Սափավովթ	Sap'avovt'	V 423 app
Սեգովր	Segovr	V 442

Սեգորով	Segorov	V 442 app.
Սեդէկիա	Sedēkia	V 439
Սեդիմ	Sedim	V 440
Սելովամ	Selovam	V 451
Սելում	Selum	V 443
Սեհոն	Sehon	V 444
Սեղովմ	Sełovm	V 445
Սեմ	Sem	V 446
Սեմէի	Semēi	V 447
Սենեքերիմ	Senēk'ērim	V 448
Սեփովրայ	Sep'ovray	V 450
Սէթ	Sēt'	V 441
Սէոն	Sēon	V 449
Սիբայ	Siba	V 452
Սիրողէթ	Sibołēt	V 453
Սիմէովն	Simēovn	V 454
Սիմոն	Simōn	V 455
Սիմ,	Sim	V 456
Սինոյն	Sinoyn	C 457 app.
Սիոն	Sion	V 457
Սիսարայ	Sisara	V 458
Սիւքեմ	Siwk'em	V 459
Սիքոր	Sik'or	V 460
Սկարիովտացի	Skariovtac'i	V 461
Սոդոմ	Sodom	V 462
Սոմեր	Somer	V 463
Սովմնացի	Sov'mnac'i	V 464
Սորեկ	Sorek	V 465
Սոփիդիմ	Sop'idim	V 466
Ստեփաննոս	Step'annos	V 467
Վաւ	Vaw	I ii 6
Վաքաբովդ	Vak'abovd	V 468
Տարսոս	Tarsos	V 469
Տեթ	Tet'	I ii 9
Տիմէոս	Timēos	V 470
Տիմոթէոս	Timot'ēos	V 471

Տիտոս	Titos	V 472
Տիւրացիք	Tiwrac'ik'	V 473
Տուբիայ	Tubiay	V 474
Րեշ	Reš	I ii 20
Ցովդ	C'ovd	I ii 10
Փակէէ	P'akēē	V 475
Փաղեկ	P'ałek	V 484
Փանուէլ	P'anuēl	V 476
Փասկա	P'aska	V 477
Փարաւոն	P'arawon	V 478
Փարէզ	P'arez	V 479
Փարիսեցիք	P'arisec'ik'	V 480
Փենէշէզ	P'enēhēz	V 481
Փէ	P'ē	I ii 17
Փոքոր	P'ok'or	V 482
Փութ	P'ut'	V 483
Քաբ	K'ab	I ii 11
Քազբի	K'azbi	V 486
Քաղդեաստան	K'ałdēastan	V 485
Քաղէբ	K'ałēb	V 487
Քամ	K'am	V 488
Քամիլ	K'amil	I ii 3
Քանան	K'anan	V 489
Քեբրոն	K'ebron	V 490
Քետուրա	K'etura	V 491
Քոր	K'or	V 492
Քորազին	K'orazin	V 494
Քորեբ	K'oreb	V 493
Քուշ	K'uš	V 495
Քուս	K'us	V 496
Քրիստոս	K'ristos	V 497

GENERAL INDEX

This index does not include proper names of manuscripts included in the lists on pages xi-xvi and 212-217. Names included in the onomastic texts published are found in the preceding Onomastic Index.